Reading CPE

Eight more practice tests for
the **Cambridge C2 Proficiency**

Introduction

Welcome to this second edition of sample tests for the Cambridge C2 Proficiency (CPE) Reading examination (Parts 5–7).

Parts 5–7 of the Reading and Use of English section test candidates' ability in reading different types of text for detail, purpose, opinion, tone and attitude, and repeated practice of the assessment format is key to achieving a passing grade.

This resource comprises eight whole Reading tests, answer keys, write-in answer sheets and a marking scheme allowing you to score each test out of 23 marks.

The content has been written to closely replicate the Cambridge exam experience, and has undergone comprehensive expert and peer review. You or your students, if you are a teacher, will hopefully enjoy the wide range of essay topics and benefit from the repetitive practice, something that is key to preparing for this section of the Cambridge C2 Proficiency (CPE) examination.

We hope that you will find this resource a useful study aid, and we wish you all the best in preparing for the exam.

Prosperity Education
Cambridge, 2023

For more Cambridge exam-preparation materials, including free sample tests and online resources, visit www.prosperityeducation.net

Cambridge C2 Proficiency Reading

Test 1

Part 5

You are going to read an extract from an article. For questions 31–36, mark the appropriate answer (A, B, C or D) that you think fits best according to the text.

Unlocking opportunities
James Pennywise describes his experience of becoming a locksmith

For me, becoming a locksmith has been a transformative journey. When I embarked on this career path, I never anticipated the vast array of challenges and fulfilling experiences that would await me. Locksmiths are responsible for installing, repairing and maintaining various types of locks, including those with mechanical and electronic systems. We also help people who cannot access their homes. Being a locksmith requires precision, attention to detail and a thorough understanding of all lock mechanisms. Nowadays, however, locksmiths specialise more and more in automotive locksmithing work, dealing with different types of vehicle locks, including traditional locks as well as 'transponder' and 'smart' locks, which are more modern types of locks. That work typically involves unlocking vehicles, making new keys and programming transponders.

My journey began with a burning curiosity for the inner workings of locks. I was always fascinated by their intricate mechanisms and the mysteries hidden behind their sturdy exteriors. To pursue my passion, I embarked on an extensive training process that involved acquiring technical knowledge and practical skills, and obtaining the necessary certifications. This training process began with my apprenticeship and continued after I had completed it. Getting a high school diploma or equivalent qualification is typically a good first step. Although not a mandatory requirement, a solid educational foundation can significantly enhance one's understanding of the field. After completing my basic education at school, I pursued specialised locksmithing courses from accredited institutions that covered various aspects of the trade, including lock installation, repair, picking and key duplication, and skills such as how to communicate effectively. I learned from locksmiths with whom I am still in contact today. As a result, I was equipped with the knowledge needed to understand the different types of locks, their vulnerabilities and the techniques used to manipulate them.

In addition to theoretical knowledge, hands-on experience is invaluable in this trade. I sought opportunities to work as an apprentice under experienced locksmiths. My apprenticeship allowed me to observe and learn from seasoned professionals so as to be able to hone my practical skills and deepen my understanding of real-life scenarios that locksmiths encounter. I was fortunate enough to learn from several elite locksmiths that I encountered during my apprenticeship. Many aspiring locksmiths seem to find an apprenticeship through their personal contacts, further adding to the profession's mystique and the idea that knowledge is well-guarded and only revealed to a chosen few. However, I didn't have that advantage and so was left no option but to go through the publicly available channels.

As a locksmith, every day is a new adventure filled with diverse challenges. One of the job's core responsibilities is to be on call and attend emergency 'lockouts' when needed. A significant portion of my work involves assisting individuals who have been locked out of their homes, cars or businesses. Responding promptly and effectively to these situations requires problem-solving skills, technical expertise and empathy for those in distress. People are usually not in the best of moods when I arrive, and to make matters worse they then have to pay out a hefty sum for the service. I don't like to feel that I have the right to demand lots of money, but this part of the job really is where locksmiths earn the majority of their money. To be honest, I think it's only fair that we get paid a fair wage, especially as when we are providing this service we might need to get out of bed in the middle of the night and race across town.

Crafting keys is another essential skill for locksmiths. Whether it's duplicating keys for customers or creating new keys when the originals are lost, this task demands precision and the ability to operate key-cutting machines accurately.

An additional aspect of the job that is very important today is security consultation. I often provide expert advice on state-of-the-art security systems and measures to protect homes, businesses or other properties. This involves assessing vulnerabilities, recommending appropriate locks, alarms and access-control systems, and educating clients on the latest security trends. Although I do not currently have any apprentices of my own to train, I would definitely be interested in pursuing that type of role at some point in the future.

Being a locksmith is not just about unlocking doors or duplicating keys; it's about being a trusted problem-solver, a reliable source of security advice and a compassionate helper in times of crisis. You will often find yourself in situations where your expertise and calm demeanour can bring immense relief to individuals facing lockouts or security concerns.

Test 1

31 What does the writer say that locksmiths do more often now than they used to?

    A repair specific types of locks

    B work on locks for cars

    C work carefully and accurately on locks

    D help people with problems with technology

32 The writer thinks that staying at school

    A is a quicker way to get an apprenticeship as a locksmith.

    B helps you to make connections with people who can help you later.

    C gives you the communication skills you need to help people that need it.

    D makes it easier for you to learn how to be a locksmith.

33 The writer thinks that he owes his skill as a locksmith today to

    A the experienced locksmiths who trained him.

    B the fact he was chosen by a top locksmith to be his apprentice.

    C help from relatives who had contacts in the industry.

    D the training programme he took part in that is available to everybody.

34 What does the writer think about how much people have to pay for 'lockouts'?

    A He understands why some people think they are paying too much.

    B He sees it as an opportunity to earn a good amount of money quickly.

    C He thinks it's necessary to charge a premium because it's a significant factor in a locksmith's income.

    D He thinks people should pay more due to the compassion with which he helps them.

35 What educational aspect of his job does the writer mention?

    A assisting people who have locked themselves out

    B training young people who are his apprentices

    C showing people the vulnerabilities of the keys he has cut for them

    D sharing knowledge of how to protect property

36 The impression given of the writer is that he

    A focuses more on the human aspects of his job than on the technical aspects.

    B sees his work as more than just a series of mechanical tasks.

    C would like to work in more hi-tech areas of locksmithing.

    D is never irritated by having to get up in the night to help people.

Part 6

You are going to read an extract from an online article. Seven paragraphs have been removed. Select from the paragraphs A–H the one that fits each gap (questions 37–43). There is one extra paragraph that you do not need to use.

Email Marketing: Using the Power of Digital Communication

In today's digital era, email marketing has emerged as a powerful tool for businesses to connect with their target audience, promote their products or services and nurture customer relationships. With its wide reach, cost-effectiveness and ability to deliver personalised content, email marketing has become an indispensable component of modern marketing strategies. Here we explore the intricacies of email marketing, its key benefits and how to effectively utilise this versatile tool to maximise results.

37

One of the primary advantages of email marketing is its vast reach. With billions of active email users worldwide, businesses can connect with a wide audience that spans different demographics, locations and interests. Unlike other marketing channels, email allows for targeted messaging, ensuring that the right message reaches the right people at the right time. By segmenting the subscriber base and tailoring content to specific audiences, marketers can significantly increase the success of their campaigns at an extremely low cost.

38

Another crucial aspect of email marketing is its ability to deliver specifically targeted content. With the help of customer data and marketing automation tools, businesses can create highly targeted emails, tailored to each recipient's preferences, behaviour and purchasing history.

39

However, it is essential to strike a balance when it comes to email frequency. While regular communication is crucial for maintaining engagement, bombarding subscribers with emails can lead to frustration and increased 'opt-out' or 'unsubscribe' rates. Finding the optimal 'tone of voice' for an email requires testing and monitoring audience responses to ensure the right balance between making an impact and avoiding the risk of being perceived as unwanted junk mail.

40

As was previously mentioned, to maximise the effectiveness of email marketing, marketers should continuously experiment with various strategies and techniques such as A/B testing for instance. This allows businesses to compare different elements of their emails, such as subject lines or images, to identify what resonates best with their audience. Email automation workflows offer unprecedented efficiency as they can be set up to deliver targeted messages at pre-defined intervals based on user actions or milestones. This, in turn, enhances customers' engagement and drives sales.

41

However, it is crucial to respect a user's right to decide what emails they receive, find the right balance in email frequency and continuously optimise and experiment with strategies to ensure long-term success. If email marketers do not do this they risk potentially being prosecuted for illegal activity or, as is more often the case, irritating potential customers to the point where they decide to unsubscribe from their company's email notifications.

42

It is important to remember that email marketing is just one piece of the larger marketing puzzle. Integrating email campaigns with other digital marketing channels, such as social media and content marketing, can amplify the overall impact of marketing efforts. Cross-promoting content, incorporating social sharing buttons in emails and driving traffic from social media to email subscription forms can create a cohesive and powerful marketing ecosystem that makes a company stand out.

43

As technology continues to evolve and consumer behaviour changes, adapting and refining email-marketing strategies will be crucial. By staying informed about the latest trends, complying with regulations and embracing innovation, businesses can harness the full power of email marketing to achieve their marketing goals and stay ahead in the competitive digital landscape.

A   Email marketing has revolutionised the effectiveness with which businesses can communicate with their customers. Its wide reach, cost-effectiveness, personalisation capabilities and potential for automation make it a multi-faceted and invaluable tool for marketers. By harnessing the power of email marketing, businesses can nurture customer relationships, drive engagement and achieve their marketing objectives.

B   Email marketing refers to the practice of sending a wide range of commercial messages to groups of people via email. These messages span promotional offers, newsletters, event invitations and product updates to personalised recommendations based on user behaviour. Its fundamental goal is to establish and maintain a relationship with the recipients, ultimately boosting engagement, brand loyalty and sales conversions and driving corporate success.

C   Moreover, compliance with privacy regulations, such as the General Data Protection Regulation (GDPR) in the UK is paramount in email marketing. These regulations ensure that businesses obtain explicit consent from recipients, provide easy opt-out mechanisms and handle personal data securely. Adhering to these guidelines not only protects the privacy of subscribers but also helps build trust and credibility in the brand.

D   Indeed, email marketing offers unparalleled cost-effectiveness. Compared to traditional marketing channels like print or television, email campaigns require minimal investment. There are no printing or postage costs involved, for instance, making it an affordable option for businesses of all sizes. Additionally, email marketing platforms provide advanced analytical and reporting tools that allow marketers to track campaign performance, measure key metrics and optimise their strategies based on data-driven insights.

E   Data collection involving third parties should involve clear guidelines regarding how the data collected in this way will be used and who owns it. Furthermore, it is essential for corporations to provide ways for users to opt-out of tracking or email marketing through visible notices. From an internal company perspective, marketing executives also need to ensure that all tracking or data-collection activities that occur do not conflict with their company's online privacy policy.

F   In today's fast-paced digital landscape, email marketing has become a cornerstone of effective communication and relationship-building between businesses and their customers of all kinds. By keeping in mind likely human reactions to messages and what people tend to respond to positively, businesses can create impactful email campaigns that customers engage with.

G   Email marketing is likely to remain a vital tool in the marketer's toolbox. Its ability to reach a wide audience, deliver personalised content and drive engagement and conversions makes it a very valuable asset for all businesses. By employing effective segmentation, personalisation, automation and regular testing, businesses can unlock its true potential and establish meaningful connections with their customers which will differentiate a company from its competitors.

H   Personalising content to the profiles and interests of specific users can serve to foster a sense of exclusivity, which makes these users feel valued and appreciated, and ultimately drives engagement and conversions. By utilising techniques like dynamic content, product recommendations and triggered emails, businesses can provide relevant and timely information to their subscribers, increasing the chances of them purchasing a product or service.

Part 7

You are going to read an extract from a newspaper article in which five art critics choose their favourite artwork. For questions 44–53, choose from the sections (A–E). The sections may be selected more than once.

In which section are the following mentioned?

the artist's ability to make us question what we assumed was real	44
being able to create a long-lasting artistic legacy	45
the ability of certain painting methods to inspire strong feelings in the viewer	46
art's ability to demonstrate that people can achieve great things	47
the relationship between people and the natural world	48
the view that art can be used as a cry of pain in a brutal world	49
an artwork's ability to create the feeling that the viewer is inside it	50
art's ability to show us how brief our time is on Earth	51
the possibility of combining art with efforts to create a fairer society	52
the artist's ability to represent the movement of a subject through the techniques they use	53

The greatest artwork of all time

A: Tristan Shannon – Arguing for 'The Starry Night' by Vincent van Gogh

Vincent Van Gogh's 'The Starry Night' is an awe-inspiring masterpiece that transcends the boundaries of traditional art. With its mesmerising depiction of the night sky, Van Gogh's use of swirling brushstrokes and vibrant colours creates a sense of enchantment and emotional depth. The artist adds texture and intensity to the painting, resulting in a three-dimensional effect that draws the viewer to the scene. 'The Starry Night' embodies Van Gogh's distinctive artistic vision and his ability to convey raw human emotions through his work. The artist's use of contrasting colours and energetic brushwork evokes a sense of movement and energy, capturing the essence of the night sky in a way that is almost spiritual. This painting is a testament to van Gogh's artistic genius and remains an enduring symbol of the power of art to evoke deep emotions and spark the imagination.

B: Sarita Sawali – Advocating for 'Mona Lisa' by Leonardo da Vinci

Leonardo da Vinci's 'Mona Lisa' stands as an enigmatic masterpiece that has captivated audiences for centuries. The painting showcases da Vinci's mastery of technique and his meticulous attention to detail, and Mona Lisa's enigmatic smile, serene gaze and the play of light and shadow all contribute to the painting's aura of intrigue and fascination. Da Vinci's use of a technique that blurs colours and tones, imparts a soft and ethereal quality to the painting. The depth and realism achieved in Mona Lisa's face, as well as the intricate details of her clothing and the landscape in the background, demonstrate da Vinci's unparalleled skill as an artist. 'Mona Lisa' represents the epitome of Renaissance art, combining a harmonious balance of naturalism, idealism and symbolism. Da Vinci's ability to capture the essence of his subject and infuse it with a sense of mystery and intrigue makes 'Mona Lisa' an enduring masterpiece that continues to captivate audiences and inspire countless artists.

C: Miguel Martinez – Making a case for 'The Persistence of Memory' by Salvador Dalí

Salvador Dalí's 'The Persistence of Memory' is a surrealist masterpiece that challenges the boundaries of reality and perception. The painting's dreamlike quality and its depiction of melting clocks and distorted landscapes provoke contemplation and intrigue. Dalí's meticulous attention to detail, combined with his imaginative symbolism, creates a world that blurs the line between fantasy and reality. The melting clocks, an iconic element of this painting, represent the fluidity and subjectivity of time. They symbolise the transient nature of existence and the futility of trying to control or grasp time. The empty landscape and the distant horizon evoke a sense of desolation and the fragility of human existence. Through his use of juxtaposition and symbolism, Dalí invites viewers to explore the depths of their own subconscious and question the nature of reality.

D: Arthur Atkins – Putting forward 'The Creation of Adam' by Michelangelo

'The Creation of Adam' by Michelangelo is an undisputed wonder that epitomises Renaissance art. Michelangelo's mastery of anatomy, proportion and perspective is on full display in this truly awe-inspiring work. The dynamic composition and the perfect symmetry of the figures showcase Michelangelo's technical brilliance and artistic vision. The intricate details of the human form, the delicate folds of fabric and the play of light and shadow reveal the artist's unparalleled skill and attention to detail. Each brushstroke and contour convey a sense of grace and power. 'The Creation of Adam' serves as a testament to the limitless potential of the human spirit at time when Europe was in the middle of war and unrest. It represents the Renaissance ideal of humanism, highlighting the belief in the individual's ability to strive for greatness and connection with God. The painting's grand scale and monumental presence further enhance its impact, enveloping the viewer in a spiritual and contemplative experience.

E: Barnie Hearsey – Proposing 'Guernica' by Pablo Picasso

'Guernica' by Pablo Picasso is a very significant work of art that serves as a powerful condemnation of the horrors of war. This monumental painting, executed in tones of grey, white and black, depicts the devastating bombing of the town of Guernica during the Spanish Civil War. Picasso's fragmented and distorted forms, combined with his bold brushwork, evoke a sense of chaos and anguish. 'Guernica' is a visual protest against the brutality and suffering inflicted upon innocent civilians. The anguished faces and frantic animals symbolise the pain and despair experienced by the victims of the bombing. The sheer emotional impact of 'Guernica' is overwhelming. Picasso's ability to capture the essence of human suffering and his bold expression of outrage make this painting a timeless masterpiece. It stands as a powerful reminder of the consequences of violence and the need for peace and compassion in our world. This painting remains an enduring symbol of protest and a call to action against the atrocities of war. Picasso's artistic genius and his constant commitment to social justice have cemented this painting as one of the most significant and influential works of art of the 20th century.

Cambridge C2 Proficiency Reading — Answer sheet

Name _____   Date _____

Part 5
Mark the appropriate answer.

0	A ☐	B ☐	C ■	D ☐
31	A ☐	B ☐	C ☐	D ☐
32	A ☐	B ☐	C ☐	D ☐
33	A ☐	B ☐	C ☐	D ☐
34	A ☐	B ☐	C ☐	D ☐
35	A ☐	B ☐	C ☐	D ☐
36	A ☐	B ☐	C ☐	D ☐

Part 6
Add the appropriate answer.

37	38	39	40	41	42	43

Part 7
Add the appropriate answer.

44	45
46	47
48	49
50	51
52	53

Cambridge C2 Proficiency Reading

Test 2

Part 5

You are going to read an extract from an article. For questions 31–36, mark the appropriate answer (A, B, C or D) that you think fits best according to the text.

An amateur violin maker

Music has always been a passion of mine, and although I can at best be described as a keen amateur, I have always played one instrument or another. Ever since I was a fresh-faced student, I have played the guitar, and prior to that I took piano and violin lessons at school. I have always loved how beautiful musical instruments look and had long promised myself that one day I would build one of my own, despite this having seemed to be a totally unrealistic prospect. I imagined it would be a guitar because that's the instrument that's closest to my heart, but things didn't quite work out that way.

I started looking online for a workshop that provided classes in instrument construction in my area, but I started to despair as nothing showed up in the many searches I made and none of my musician friends could help me either. However, I did find the number for a chap called Tony Marcos who is a luthier. No sooner had I looked up the meaning of 'luthier' – which means 'violin maker' – than I was writing an email to Tony to ask if he still had any spaces available on his violin-building course, which runs from June to September every year. He told me that there really weren't any luthiers specialising in acoustic guitars within the area. So desperate was I to get on with my new course of study, I decided that making a violin would do just fine.

Attending the course was, from the off, a transformative experience that deepened my appreciation for the craftsmanship and artistry involved in creating musical instruments even further. Over the duration of the course, my fellow students and I embarked on a journey of discovery in which we faced numerous challenges and learned an incredible amount about the intricacies of violin making.

We began with the design phase, where we delved into the dimensions and proportions of the instrument, considering factors such as the instrument's sound and playability. What really astounded me was discovering that the careful selection of materials, such as spruce wood for the top plate and maple wood for the back, ribs and neck, plays a crucial role in achieving the desired sound that the instrument makes. Tony was an incredible teacher who taught us to visualise our designs and showed us how to use the appropriate equipment to translate our ideas into a detailed plan. This then served as a blueprint throughout the construction process.

The building phase involves shaping and carving the various components of the violin. The top plate, back plate, ribs and scroll are meticulously crafted according to precise measurements, ensuring optimal acoustic properties and structural integrity. Techniques such as 'purfling' – the delicate process of inlaying decorative strips around the edges – not only enhance the visual appeal but also strengthen the instrument.

We encountered numerous difficulties throughout the process. You need to handle the wood very careful so that it does not crack. You need a steady hand and a deep understanding of the shape of the instrument to carve it correctly. What's more, the selection of varnish and its application to the wood to preserve it and make it shine demands technical expertise and a sense of how to make objects look attractive. Additionally, positioning the parts of the instrument in the right place to optimise the instrument's sound can prove particularly challenging. Patience, perseverance and a commitment to craftsmanship proved to be essential in overcoming these obstacles.

My instrument finally began to look like it might be finished by the end of the course. However, I had my doubts. I will never forget the first time I attached the strings and played it with the bow I had brought from home. It was an almost ceremonial moment for me. Tony was there and I'm sure he understood my excitement. He did give me some good advice on improving the sound, but he was kind enough to wait until the next class, and just let me appreciate what I had achieved for a couple of days. I treated myself to a beautiful modern case for my creation and took it home. I have hardly put the instrument down since.

Attending the violin-making course gave me a comprehensive understanding of the artistry and technical skill involved in crafting a violin. It proved, for me, to be a true labour of love. However, I would say that what we learned was just the tip of the iceberg in terms of the knowledge and skills required to pursue a passion for violin making professionally. I'm still over the moon with my effort though, and I will cherish the violin and the experience forever.

Test 2

31 What is the writer's experience of playing musical instruments?

  A He has concentrated on playing just one instrument.
  B He has played several instruments but likes one the most.
  C He has always loved music, but creating his own music isn't for him.
  D He has done it from time to time over the years when he could.

32 How did the writer find the course that he did?

  A after doing extensive research of available courses
  B the course leader contacted him
  C by posting a request for help online
  D the course leader was a friend of a friend

33 What was the most important thing that the writer learned in the design phase?

  A how to imagine what your ideas will look like
  B how to use accurate measuring tools
  C how to ensure you have the correct measurements
  D how to choose appropriate resources

34 In which part of the process can violin builders express themselves artistically?

  A designing the correct shape for the instrument
  B the carving of the instrument
  C the application of varnish to the instrument
  D the attaching of the violin's parts

35 How did the writer's teacher react to the completion of his instrument?

  A He was keen to point out the areas for improvement he noticed.
  B He complimented the writer on his achievement.
  C He was excited his student had finished.
  D He gave careful thought to the feedback he gave him on it.

36 How does the writer feel at the end of the course?

  A He feels he has reached the end of his violin-building journey.
  B He still has a lot to learn about how to build violins.
  C He enjoyed it, but he isn't completely satisfied with his violin.
  D He is already planning to take further courses to develop his skills.

Part 6

You are going to read an extract from a magazine article. Seven paragraphs have been removed. Select from the paragraphs A–H the one that fits each gap (questions 37–43). There is one extra paragraph that you do not need to use.

How to have a thriving career as a super car journalist

Mark Thompson, a renowned automotive journalist at *Super Car Magazine*, has crafted a remarkable career fuelled by his lifelong obsession with cars. From an early age, Mark's love of automobiles paved the way for a thrilling journey that led him to test-drive and review some of the world's most exotic vehicles. This is his captivating story of discovery, which traces how his constant love for cars unfolded into his dream job.

37

As Mark entered his teenage years, his passion for cars evolved into a serious pursuit. He decided to try go-karting, where he discovered the thrill of high-speed racing and developed a profound understanding of vehicle dynamics. It was during these formative years that his appreciation for performance and precision took root, setting the stage for his future endeavours.

38

"We didn't have too much money, but there were a lot of rich parents coming to the races where their kids were driving. Most of them were motor enthusiasts, just like us. However, they had the means to be able to drive fancy luxury cars. I loved to ask questions and sit in these cars. I was a bit obsessed with it, really. I just loved knowing everything about a car."

39

Mark's talent and unique approach did not go unnoticed, and caught the attention of television producers. They invited him to collaborate on a TV programme centred around supercars, which opened up exciting opportunities for his increasingly successful career. His ability to convey the essence of each car he encountered, along with his infectious enthusiasm, captivated viewers and propelled him to become a sought-after automotive personality.

40

"It really was a dream come true. I had to pinch myself sometimes. I used to become so excited the night before I'd test a new car that I found it hard to get to sleep. I would use the time to plan my reports to try to make them stand out from all the other motor reviews you see on the internet or TV. I would turn up for the test a bit tired, but always meticulously well prepared. I'm so pleased that viewers noticed the extra mile I went to prepare for my job. It has been a tremendous help in my early career and really catapulted me to bigger and better things."

41

Among the remarkable cars he has driven, one holds a special place in Mark's heart – the iconic McLaren F1. "Its ground-breaking design, incredible performance and unparalleled driving experience make it my all-time favourite. The F1's symphony of engineering brilliance, combined with the emotional connection it creates with the driver, embodies the true essence of automotive passion."

42

Beyond the glitz and glamour of the supercar world, Mark's career has also taught him the importance of responsible journalism. He understands that with great influence comes great responsibility. Thus, he strives to deliver unbiased and honest reviews in order to provide valuable information to assist consumers in making informed decisions about their dream machines.

43

A Throughout his illustrious career, Mark has had the privilege of getting behind the wheel of numerous automotive masterpieces, each leaving an indelible mark on his soul. Whether it's the heart-pounding acceleration and sheer opulence of the Bugatti Chiron or the mind-boggling top speed and uncompromising aerodynamics of the Koenigsegg Jesko Absolut, every car has its own story to tell. Mark's ability to articulate the distinct characteristics of each vehicle has cemented his reputation as an authority in the industry.

B It was a great coincidence when Mark's path intersected with individuals who owned exquisite and luxurious cars at a young age. He explains, "My father was a mechanic, and when I was a kid, I used to do karting, using a kart dad had done up in his spare time. I dreamed of being an F1 driver one day and I was actually quite good. I managed to win some things and our team moved up the categories each year as I grew up."

C Mark's journey from an avid car enthusiast to a respected automotive journalist at *Super Car Magazine* has been a thrilling ride. His dedication to the technological and emotional aspects of driving have allowed him to excel in his craft. Hours of meticulous research and preparation precede every review, ensuring that his articles are informative, engaging and accurate.

D Acquiring all this knowledge and hearing so many fascinating stories inspired Mark to share his own experiences and insights. Armed with a burning desire to connect with fellow enthusiasts, he created a personal blog and YouTube channel through which he chronicled his automotive adventures. Through his engaging writing style and charismatic on-screen presence, Mark captivated an audience and gained recognition within the automotive community.

E However, Mark has not received a universally positive response to his career choice from those around him. There are people who feel that automobile journalism is not a suitably serious form of journalism and that Mark should be using his training to highlight issues such as social inequalities or damage to the environment and thus raise awareness of these problems amongst the public. Super car journalism can seem like it's purely an indulgence.

F With an insatiable thirst for knowledge and a devotion to automobiles, Mark's passion for cars had emerged at a very early stage and stayed with him for decades to come. Having grown up in a small town, he had read countless automotive magazines, enjoying every article and meticulously memorising car models and specifications. His parents often found him engrossed in detailed drawings of sports cars, dreaming of one day experiencing the exhilaration of being behind the wheel.

G As Mark's career soared, he embarked on extensive travels to attend international motor shows and automotive events. These journeys took him to destinations far and wide, offering exclusive access to the world's most impressive cars. From the sun-soaked streets of Maranello to the iconic Nürburgring Nordschleife, he experienced the ultimate form of automotive excellence first-hand.

H Mark envisions an automotive landscape characterised by constant innovation and transformation and this is the message he seeks to communicate. With the rise of electric supercars and the integration of advanced autonomous driving technologies, he anticipates an exciting era of unparalleled performance and sustainability. Mark's enormous curiosity and adaptability ensure that he remains at the forefront of automotive journalism, providing invaluable insights into these ground-breaking developments.

Cambridge C2 Proficiency Reading

Part 7

You are going to read an extract from an article in which five experts share insights about the past, present and future of human contact with Mars. For questions 44–53, choose from the sections (A–E). The sections may be selected more than once.

In which section are the following mentioned?

the timeframe for the possibility of people being on Mars	44
the technical requirements that need to be fulfilled to allow people to achieve a goal	45
the conviction that another planet could affect what happens on Earth	46
attempts to establish how feasible it would be for people to live on Mars	47
plans to analyse geological samples from Mars on Earth	48
artistic representations of life on Mars	49
the ancient religious connections that Mars has	50
the factors affecting the chances of achieving a scientific goal	51
showing that a long-held belief about Mars is not true	52
an interest in rock formations on Mars and the planet's composition	53

The Past, Present and Future of Martian Exploration:
Unravelling the Red Planet's Mysteries and Potential for Humanity

The quest to comprehend Mars has fascinated humanity for decades. Here we explore the past, present and future of Martian exploration with contributions from experts in these respective fields.

A

The name 'Mars' has its origins in Roman mythology. Over two thousand years ago, the Romans named the planet after their god of war, Mars, who was considered the counterpart to the Greek god Ares. Mars was associated with aggression, strength and military prowess, making it a fitting name for the red planet that appeared fiery and intense in the night sky. That reddish hue is caused by iron oxide (rust) on its surface, by the way. Mars was considered at that time a symbol of masculine energy and was frequently depicted in artwork and mythology. The Ancient Egyptians also identified Mars in their celestial observations. They referred to the planet as 'Horus the Red', associating it with their falcon-headed god, Horus, who represented the sky and kingship. Mars played a central role in Egyptian astrology and religious beliefs, as its movements were believed to hold divine messages and influence human affairs.

B

Humanity has long been captivated by the idea of Martians and 'little green men'. These concepts gained popularity in the past, particularly during the golden age of science fiction in the mid-20th century. The distant appeal of Mars became a fertile ground for imaginative speculations. From H.G. Wells' *War of the Worlds* to Ray Bradbury's *The Martian Chronicles*, Mars became a backdrop for thrilling tales of alien civilisations, daring expeditions and encounters with extra-terrestrial beings. The notion of Martians, often depicted as intelligent and advanced beings, fascinated the public's imagination and fuelled greater interest in the prospect of life beyond Earth. These imaginative depictions of Mars and its possible inhabitants shaped the popular perception of the red planet and contributed to its enduring status as a symbol of extra-terrestrial exploration and the mysteries of the universe. As we became more scientifically capable in the second half of the 20th century, we were able to get a better look at the surface of Mars and the reality of what we might find there. While this scientific approach may have disappointed alien hunters, it ushered in a new era of exploration of this distant world.

C

The first successful fly-by missions by Mariner 4 took place in 1965. The Viking programme, with the successful landing of Viking 1 and 2 in 1976, marked a significant milestone in this endeavour. These space craft conducted experiments to analyse the Martian soil and search for signs of life. Subsequently, the Sojourner rover (1997) and its successors, Spirit and Opportunity (2004), demonstrated the capability of rovers to travel across the Martian surface and conduct scientific investigations. The Mars Science Laboratory mission, with the Curiosity rover (2012), further expanded our understanding of Mars' geology, climate and the possibility of humans living on it. This was followed by the Insight lander (2018), which focused on studying the planet's interior structure. These accomplishments paved the way for more ambitious explorations and propelled Mars exploration to new heights. Launched in 2020, NASA's Perseverance rover represents the latest mission to Mars. Equipped with advanced scientific instruments and a ground-breaking sample-caching system, it aims to search for signs of very small-scale past life, collect samples for potential return to Earth and test technologies for future explorative missions that could involve colonisation. China's Tianwen-1 mission, which also launched in 2020, consists of an orbiter, a lander and a rover. The mission's rover, Zhurong, will explore the surface of the planet, playing special attention to its rocks and soil.

D

NASA, in collaboration with the European Space Agency (ESA), plans to launch the Mars Sample Return mission in the 2030s. This endeavour aims to collect samples gathered by the Perseverance rover and return them to Earth, enabling detailed laboratory examination and potentially confirming the presence of ancient Martian life. Of course, space missions to Mars with human crews have received much attention in recent decades, but no such mission has yet taken place. Multiple space agencies, including NASA and private companies like SpaceX, have expressed intentions to send humans to Mars in the future. Although a definitive timeline remains uncertain, preliminary plans suggest that human missions may occur within the next two to three decades.

E

Successful colonisation would only be possible if there were sustainable life-support systems, efficient resource utilisation, and a reduction of the negative effects of the hostile Martian environment, including radiation and extreme temperatures. Additionally, the establishment of long-term habitats and self-sustaining ecosystems would be vital for sustained human presence. Colonising Mars represents an extraordinary endeavour with formidable challenges. However, recent technological advancements and accumulated knowledge from Martian exploration have increased the chance of achieving this ambitious goal. The chances of success ultimately depend on addressing critical factors. Advancements in robotics, life support systems and resource-utilisation technologies have paved the way for potential projects. Additionally, ongoing research in areas such as 3D printing, renewable energy and closed-loop ecosystems offers promising avenues for sustaining human presence on Mars. International cooperation allows for shared expertise, resources and financial support, increasing the likelihood of overcoming challenges and accelerating progress.

Cambridge C2 Proficiency Reading

Answer sheet

Name _____   Date _____

Part 5
Mark the appropriate answer.

0	A ☐	B ☐	C ■	D ☐
31	A ☐	B ☐	C ☐	D ☐
32	A ☐	B ☐	C ☐	D ☐
33	A ☐	B ☐	C ☐	D ☐
34	A ☐	B ☐	C ☐	D ☐
35	A ☐	B ☐	C ☐	D ☐
36	A ☐	B ☐	C ☐	D ☐

Part 6
Add the appropriate answer.

37	38	39	40	41	42	43

Part 7
Add the appropriate answer.

44	45
46	47
48	49
50	51
52	53

Cambridge C2 Proficiency Reading

Test 3

Part 5

You are going to read an extract from an article. For questions 31–36, mark the appropriate answer (A, B, C or D) that you think fits best according to the text.

The Waverley

The Waverley paddle steamboat, with its rich history and long-lasting appeal, represents a magnificent reminder of what maritime travel was like in the past. As a historical enthusiast, it brings me great joy to dive into the captivating story of this remarkable vessel and share its intriguing secrets.

The Waverley was built in 1946 by A. & J. Inglis in Glasgow, Scotland, and was originally commissioned for the London and Northeastern Railway (LNER) to provide pleasure cruises along the Firth of Clyde. Named after Sir Walter Scott's novel, it embodied the spirit of adventure and romance that Scott's literary works so elegantly captured. Measuring an impressive 239 feet in length and powered by a mighty steam engine, the Waverley swiftly became a beloved sight on the Scottish waters. Its grandeur and elegance attracted both locals and tourists alike to take a ride on it and it offered them a unique experience that blended nostalgic charm with breath-taking coastal views.

One cannot discuss the appeal of the Waverley without mentioning its remarkable longevity. Despite the decline of steam-powered vessels in the mid-20th century and the fact that travel by this mode of transport clearly is not as popular as it once was, this paddle steamer defied the odds, sailing on to become the last seagoing paddle steamer in the world. Though critics today may argue that paddle-steamers are not very ecologically sound, The Waverley's ability to withstand the test of time is the direct result of its creators' craftsmanship and excellence as engineers. Rarely has the vessel succumbed to any mechanic failures.

Although the Waverley is an engineering marvel, its enduring popularity stems from its ability to transport passengers back in time, inspiring a sense of nostalgia as it reminds people of a simpler age where the pace of life was much slower and there seemed to be more time to simply enjoy oneself. It is easy to see why the vessel captures the imaginations of all who step aboard. The rhythmic movement of the paddle wheels, the gentle hiss of steam and the enchanting whistles all combine to create a multi-sensory experience that reminds passengers of a past era. Passengers have the opportunity to relive the elegance and grandeur of steamship travel, experiencing the sights, sounds and scents first-hand.

Of course, no historical tale is complete without some amusing stories. One such story revolves around an incident during the Waverley's early days. Legend has it that a mischievous seagull, known as 'Captain McWings', developed a fondness for sitting on the vessel's chimney, often causing minor delays. Passengers, amused by this bird's courage, would place bets on when Captain McWings would make his appearance. It became a popular on-board pastime, with passengers eagerly scanning the horizon in anticipation of the notorious gull.

Looking at the facts and figures, the Waverley boasts an impressive passenger capacity of 860, making it one of the largest paddle steamers ever built in Britain. Its top speed is an impressive 18 knots, allowing for swift and enjoyable voyages along the picturesque Scottish coastline. Over the years, the Waverley has covered an astonishing distance, equivalent to circling the Earth over 40 times. This unique and remarkable achievement truly highlights the vessel's unwavering dedication to providing memorable experiences to countless travellers.

As a history enthusiast, the Waverley holds a special place in my heart. For me, the most heart-warming thing is the memories this piece of Scottish history evokes. I have seen the Waverley sailing up and down the waterways of my country throughout my life. One of my earliest and fondest memories is my first voyage on the ship, with my grandparents, when I was just a small boy. Last year I took my own grandson for his first trip on the vessel. I hope it is a memory he will grow with, just as I have done. To me, the Waverley feels likes a constant source of pride for every Scot, and a testament to a now, much reduced, ship-building industry. It serves as a living monument to the genius of its creators and the enduring charm of steam-powered vessels. With every voyage, the Waverley continues to capture the hearts of those fortunate enough to step aboard, preserving the magic of years gone by for generations to come.

31 What was the original purpose of the Waverley?

   A   to fill a gap in a rail service
   B   to demonstrate Scotland's technical expertise
   C   to make its passengers feel nostalgic for the past
   D   to honour a famous Scottish writer

32 In what way has The Waverley not conformed with people's expectations?

   A   the number of technical issues that it has survived
   B   the way it still remains popular despite copies of its style
   C   the sheer length of time that it has continued to operate
   D   the impact that its steam has on the environment

33 According to the writer, what are the passengers on The Waverley yearning for?

   A   a break from the speed of contemporary life
   B   insights into the steam paddler as an engineering wonder
   C   knowledge about the history of steam-powered vessels
   D   the relaxing effects of the sounds from the vessel

34 What happened after the appearance of a notorious bird?

   A   passengers were irritated whenever it caused a delay
   B   passengers did their best to avoid it
   C   passengers were keen to see it again
   D   passengers encouraged the bird to return

35 According to the writer, the Waverley's greatest achievement is

   A   its speed.
   B   the extent to which it has travelled.
   C   the number of passengers it can carry.
   D   its preservation of very old parts of a ship.

36 What feature of the Waverley most appeals to the writer?

   A   its long and fascinating history
   B   its close connections with his home
   C   its technical excellence
   D   its ability to change with the times

Part 6

You are going to read an extract from a newspaper article. Seven paragraphs have been removed. Select from the paragraphs A–H the one that fits each gap (questions 37–43). There is one extra paragraph that you do not need to use.

The coronation of King Charles III
A review by a loyal servant

In a historic moment filled with glamour, deep symbolism and a little bit of magic, King Charles III was officially crowned, marking the start of a new era for the United Kingdom. The much-anticipated coronation ceremony, held at Westminster Abbey, captivated the attention of princes and princesses, world leaders, celebrities and millions of spectators worldwide.

| 37 | |

The coronation is full of centuries-old traditions, and it begins with a regal procession through the streets of London. Thousands of well-wishers, from all over the world, lined the route of the procession, waving Union flags and cheering enthusiastically as the newly crowned King Charles made his way to the coronation venue. The melody of a royal fanfare played on trumpets filled the air and was accompanied by the rhythmic beats of the military horses in the Household Cavalry. This all created an atmosphere of anticipation and reverence.

| 38 | |

Next came the presentation of the symbols of authority. The orb, which is a golden ball representing the monarch's rule over the world, was placed in King Charles III's hands, signifying his responsibility to protect and govern. The sceptre, a long golden staff with stunning jewels in it, was then placed in his right hand, symbolising his authority and wisdom to rule with justice and compassion. The high point of the ceremony came as the Crown of St. Edward, an awe-inspiring masterpiece of a crown with priceless gems in it, was brought forward by the Archbishop of Canterbury. With the weight of history resting upon it, the crown was carefully placed upon King Charles III's head. This created a breath-taking moment that reminded the nation of its long history and traditions. The crown symbolises the continuity of the monarchy, connecting the present sovereign with kings and queens who have come before.

| 39 | |

"I stand before you today humbled and honoured to accept the immense responsibility of leading this great nation," proclaimed King Charles III, his voice filled with conviction. "Together, we will navigate the challenges of our time, cherishing the richness of our history while embracing progress and innovation. I pledge to uphold the principles of democracy, sustainability, and compassion as we strive to build a better world for generations to come."

| 40 | |

The event is also an opportunity for the royal family to exhibit their unity and resilience. Queen Consort Camilla stood proudly by King Charles III's side, looking elegant and graceful, as a symbol of constant support for him. The presence of other members of the royal family, including William, Prince of Wales, and Catherine, Princess of Wales, along with Prince Harry, Duke of Sussex, reinforced the royal family's unity and dedication to their role as representatives of the nation.

| 41 | |

King Charles III's reign is expected to be characterised by a deep sense of duty as he endeavours to find its place amidst the complexities of the 21st century. The monarch, known for his dedication to environmental causes and his passion for promoting sustainable practices, is set to play a vital role in addressing important issues such as climate change and conservation. His commitment to public service, charitable undertakings and support for cultural and educational institutions positions him as a figurehead who can inspire and drive forward positive change within the UK.

| 42 | |

As the ceremony drew to a close, the newly crowned monarch and the royal family emerged onto the balcony of Buckingham Palace. Greeted by an ocean of well-wishers, their loud cheers echoed through the streets, showing the public's support and enthusiasm for the monarchy. The scene captured the essence of unity and shared celebration, as the nation stood together to welcome a new chapter in its history.

| 43 | |

A In his coronation speech, the delivery of which is also part of an ancient royal tradition, King Charles III expressed his profound appreciation to the British people for their support and faith in his ability to fulfil his duties. He acknowledged the challenges that lie ahead and spoke passionately about his commitment to public service and his vision for a harmonious and prosperous future.

B Despite these efforts, it would be foolish to assume that everyone in the United Kingdom is wholeheartedly behind the monarchy, and the coronation of King Charles III also provides an opportunity for reflection on the continued relevance of the British monarchy. Throughout its long history, however, the institution has faced challenges and has evolved to meet these. The transition from Queen Elizabeth II's remarkable reign to King Charles III's era signals a seamless transition of power and the continuation of a cherished institution that people both in the United Kingdom and around the world feel connected to.

C Under the camera lenses and amidst the magnificent setting of the coronation venue, King Charles III promised his constant and lifelong commitment to the nation and its people. The king vowed to carry on the legacy of his predecessors and uphold the values that have defined the British monarchy for centuries.

D Furthermore, King Charles III's reign is anticipated to witness the continuation of the royal family's charitable activities and their commitment to various causes. Building upon the work of his predecessors, he will seek to use the influence of the monarchy to raise awareness and promote initiatives that aim to improve the lives of individuals and communities.

E With the coronation of King Charles III, the United Kingdom embarks on a new era with a sense of togetherness presided over by a monarch who embodies tradition, compassion and a vision for a better future. As he assumes the weighty responsibilities of his role, the nation and the world watch with anticipation, eager to witness the impact and legacy of a reign that promises to confront the challenges of the future while honouring the past.

F The words of the monarch are a reminder of his role as the head of state in the United Kingdom. Accordingly, Charles's coronation ceremony attracted many heads of state and this underlines the significance of the event on a global scale. Leaders from across the Commonwealth, European Union and beyond sent their congratulations and expressed their commitment to fostering strong ties with the United Kingdom during King Charles III's reign.

G The coronation of King Charles III was not only about the royal family and the support they offer to each other on special occasions – it also provided an opportunity to celebrate and showcase the rich cultural heritage of the United Kingdom. The ceremony incorporated elements from various traditions and centuries-old rituals, creating a captivating spectacle that represented both tradition and modernity. The significance of the coronation extended beyond the ceremonial aspects. It represented a moment of continuity and stability in a rapidly changing world. As the United Kingdom faces complex domestic and global challenges, the monarchy assumes a unifying role, going beyond political divisions and fostering a sense of national identity and pride.

H Inside the awe-inspiring magnificent coronation hall, which was filled with beautiful decorations and illuminated by countless chandeliers, the Archbishop of Canterbury presided over the religious ceremony. King Charles III knelt before the ornate altar, surrounded by the leaders of the Church of England. With reverence and devotion, the archbishop puts sacred oil on the king's head to symbolise his divine authority.

Cambridge C2 Proficiency Reading

Part 7

You are going to read an extract from a newspaper article in which five people describe their food-budgeting methods. For questions 44–53, choose from the sections (A–E). The sections may be selected more than once.

In which section are the following mentioned?

using technology, amongst other things, to compare food items	44
structured and conscious food preparation	45
the need to know how to avoid food-related illnesses	46
a lack of loyalty to one particular food retailer	47
a method that brings the greatest financial benefits when it is used long-term	48
not needing to devote as much time to food shopping as one otherwise would	49
the psychological effects of using a specific method	50
using information from a combination of print materials and the internet	51
the distribution of food amongst a connected group of people	52
how to combat the additional expense of spontaneous purchases	53

Food budgeting

Five people tell us about different approaches to getting their weekly food shopping.

A: Freeganism

As a devoted advocate of 'freeganism', I wholeheartedly embrace a unique approach to food budgeting that focuses on minimising waste and maximising resourcefulness. For me, it is a lifestyle choice aimed at reducing my ecological footprint while keeping my expenses in check. Instead of succumbing to the lure of consumerism, I actively seek out discarded food items that are still perfectly edible but have been put in waste bins nevertheless. Through activities such as collecting edible food from waste bins and participating in food-sharing networks, I am able to obtain a fantastic range of nourishment that would otherwise go to waste. My commitment to freeganism requires a keen eye for understanding the difference between spoiled food and food that can be eaten, thus ensuring that I consume only safe and healthy provisions. By reframing my perception of waste and adopting a resourceful mindset, I am able to enjoy fewer limitations on the food I can eat. This approach also fosters a profound sense of belonging to a community of freegans who stay in touch with and support each other.

B: Coupons

As a clever practitioner of the art of using coupons to save money on food – also known as couponing – I have honed my skills in the pursuit of effective food budgeting. Armed with a range of meticulously collected and organised coupons, I embark on my shopping ventures with a steady determination to extract maximum value from every penny spent. My tireless efforts in looking through newspapers, magazines and online platforms enable me to benefit from numerous discounts, special offers and promotional deals. With a discerning eye for strategic savings, I meticulously plan my grocery shopping list to align with the available coupons. By skilfully combining these tangible vouchers with ongoing store discounts, I am able to obtain as many price reductions as possible at the checkout counter. Such careful planning translates into tangible monetary savings that accumulate over time, enabling me to stretch my food budget far beyond the limits that would otherwise be on it.

C: Bulk buying

The art of bulk buying has become my hallmark when it comes to smart food budgeting. By purchasing wholesale quantities of food, I am able to achieve substantial savings while maintaining well-stocked food cupboards. I recognise that economies of scale can allow me to secure essential food items, things that don't go off for a long time, and household necessities at significantly reduced prices. In my quest for the best savings, I meticulously compare prices and seek out wholesale suppliers, whether online or at brick-and-mortar establishments. By purchasing larger quantities of goods, I am not only able to negotiate better deals but also reduce the frequency of my shopping trips, which saves me both time and money. However, the rewards of my bulk-buying endeavours are, above all, enhanced cost efficiency and peace of mind. I know that my provisions are readily available at a fraction of the regular cost.

D: Shopping around

I diligently practise the art of shopping around to master the realm of food budgeting. Rather than succumbing to the convenience of shopping at a single store, I enjoy the adventure of exploring multiple establishments in pursuit of the best deals and the most favourable prices. Armed with a discerning eye and a carefully compiled shopping list, I make my way around the bustling aisles and vibrant marketplaces, adeptly comparing prices, scrutinising quality and weighing up the overall value offered. Through this relentless pursuit of amazing savings, I am able to capitalise on the dynamic nature of the food market. By keeping my finger on the pulse of prevailing prices and staying informed about discounts and promotions, I can artfully coordinate my purchases to secure the most advantageous deals. I am not only limited to physical stores but also love the convenience and accessibility of online platforms. By making use of the internet, I can effortlessly compare prices across various retailers, read customer reviews and make informed decisions that align with my budgetary goals.

E: Meal planning

One effective approach to food budgeting is meal planning. This involves carefully designing and organising your meals for a specific period of time, such as a week or a month. This method allows you to make the most of your budget by efficiently utilising ingredients and minimising waste. When practising meal planning, start by creating a menu for the desired time frame. Consider the number of meals you need to prepare and the dietary requirements of your household members. Next, make a detailed grocery list based on the planned meals, taking stock of the ingredients you already have at home to avoid unnecessary purchases. Meal planning provides several benefits beyond budgeting. By having a clear plan in advance, you can shop for ingredients in bulk, taking advantage of cost-effective options and discounts. Additionally, it helps to eliminate the costs associated with impulsive purchases and minimises food waste, as you only buy what you truly need. To further improve your meal planning, consider incorporating versatile ingredients that can be used in multiple dishes. This allows you to stretch your budget even further and create diverse meals from a limited number of items.

Cambridge C2 Proficiency Reading — Answer sheet

Name _____   Date _____

Part 5
Mark the appropriate answer.

| 0 | A ☐ | B ☐ | C ▬ | D ☐ |

31	A ☐	B ☐	C ☐	D ☐
32	A ☐	B ☐	C ☐	D ☐
33	A ☐	B ☐	C ☐	D ☐
34	A ☐	B ☐	C ☐	D ☐
35	A ☐	B ☐	C ☐	D ☐
36	A ☐	B ☐	C ☐	D ☐

Part 6
Add the appropriate answer.

| 37 | 38 | 39 | 40 | 41 | 42 | 43 |

Part 7
Add the appropriate answer.

44	45
46	47
48	49
50	51
52	53

Cambridge C2 Proficiency Reading

Test 4

Part 5

You are going to read an extract from an article. For questions 31–36, mark the appropriate answer (A, B, C or D) that you think fits best according to the text.

Unlocking the Power Within: Exploring Four Martial Arts Disciplines

Martial arts, with their rich history and array of disciplines, have captivated enthusiasts around the world for centuries. Each martial art offers its own unique blend of physical and mental challenges.

Karate, originating in Okinawa, Japan, is a striking-based martial art that emphasises powerful punches, kicks and knee strikes. The word 'Karate' literally translates as 'empty hand', signifying its focus on unarmed combat. With its roots in ancient martial traditions, Karate developed into a disciplined art form that cultivates both physical and mental strength. Karatekas, practitioners of Karate, undergo rigorous training to enhance their focus, discipline and self-defence skills. They practise *kata*, which are choreographed patterns of movements, and take part in one-on-one fights to develop their techniques in a practical context. As a result of this training, Karatekas gain self-confidence.

Taekwondo, originating in Korea, is renowned for its dynamic kicks and fast-paced movements. Founded in the mid-20th century, Taekwondo has become one of the most popular martial arts globally. It places great emphasis on the development of character, fostering values such as courtesy, integrity, perseverance, self-control and indomitable spirit. Taekwondo practitioners, called taekwondoists, focus on high spinning kicks and rapid footwork. This martial art also incorporates hand strikes, blocks and throws. *Poomsae*, which are sequences of movements, are practised to enhance precision and fluidity, while one-on-one fights allow taekwondoists to apply their techniques in a controlled environment. Taekwondo cultivates not only physical agility and flexibility, but also mental discipline and respect for others.

Judo, which originated in Japan in the late 19th century, is a grappling-based martial art that emphasises throws, joint locks and ground control. Founded by Jigoro Kano, 'Judo' means 'gentle way' and embodies the principle of using an opponent's energy against them. Judokas – practitioners of Judo – learn to leverage balance, timing and technique to execute precise throws and immobilise opponents on the ground. Judo training encompasses both standing techniques, known as *nage-waza*, and ground techniques, referred to as *ne-waza*. The philosophy of mutual benefit and maximum efficiency is deeply ingrained in Judo, promoting humility, self-improvement and strong mental fortitude.

Brazilian Jiu-Jitsu (BJJ), rooted in Japanese Jiu-Jitsu, emerged in the early 20th century and has gained significant popularity for its ground-based combat techniques. BJJ places a strong emphasis on positional dominance, holds and effective ground fighting. Its practitioners, known as grapplers, learn a comprehensive set of moves where you lock your opponent into one position or hold their throat or you use escape tactics to manipulate your opponent's body and prevent them from attacking you. BJJ training involves one-on-one fighting, drilling techniques and positional exercises to develop problem-solving skills, adaptability and mental resilience. One of the fundamental principles of BJJ is that smaller individuals can overcome larger opponents through technique and leverage.

While Karate and Taekwondo both fall under the umbrella of striking-based martial arts, their approaches differ significantly. Karatekas aim to generate power through strong punches and kicks, focusing on delivering devastating blows to their opponents. Taekwondoists, on the other hand, prioritise speed, flexibility and agility, and employ kicks and rapid footwork to maintain distance and overwhelm their opponents. Both arts promote discipline, mental focus and physical fitness, but their emphasis and execution differ.

Similarly, Judo and Brazilian Jiu-Jitsu share a common ground in grappling techniques, yet their approaches and objectives differ. Judo focuses on throws and quick takedowns, utilising an opponent's energy and weight to gain control. It emphasises standing techniques and the efficient use of energy to achieve victory. Judo also incorporates ground techniques to get your opponent on the mat and holds to keep them on the mat once they are there, but the primary focus remains throws and rapid transitions. On the other hand, Brazilian Jiu-Jitsu places a greater emphasis on ground fighting. BJJ practitioners aim to gain superior positions on the ground, utilising lock holds, choke holds and positional control to submit opponents. They also learn to neutralise and overcome opponents, even when facing larger and stronger adversaries. The art highlights technique, timing and using your opponent's weight against them as the keys to victory.

31 The writer's description of Taekwondo is that it helps practitioners to

   A remember complex sequences of movements.

   B learn how to promote the welfare of others.

   C develop flowing movements.

   D become psychologically stronger.

32 Why does the more energetic fighter not necessarily triumph in Judo?

   A these fighters don't always know how to achieve maximum efficiency

   B so much of the fighting takes place on the ground

   C these fighters may have a disadvantage compared to heavier fighters

   D fighters can use techniques to utilise opponents' power against them

33 In what respect are problem-solving skills useful in BJJ?

   A fighters need to know how to keep an opponent in a hold or get out of their grip

   B fighters need to know how to get out of positions on the mat and start moving again

   C fighters need to know how to approach an opponent without being seen by them

   D fighters need to know how to overcome obstacles to move from standing positions to a position on the mat

34 The writer suggests that the most significant difference between Karate and Taekwondo is

   A how much time practitioners spend on the ground while fighting.

   B how practitioners solve problems while fighting against one other person.

   C how practitioners gain an advantage over their opponents.

   D how frequently practitioners change their position while fighting.

35 According to the writer, what do Judo and BJJ practitioners both do?

   A try to make use of their opponents' energy to gain an advantage over them

   B try to get their opponents to remain standing up for as long as possible

   C try to get their opponents on the ground as quickly as possible

   D try to get a hold of their opponents so that they can't move

36 What sets Karate apart from all the other martial arts the writer mentions?

   A the one-on-one practice fights its practitioners engage in

   B the fact that it can trace its origins back the furthest

   C the fast movements that its practitioners make

   D the way it combines kicks with punches

Part 6

You are going to read an extract from a newspaper article. Seven paragraphs have been removed. Select from the paragraphs A–H the one that fits each gap (questions 37–43). There is one extra paragraph that you do not need to use.

Pirates or patriots?

Throughout history, certain individuals have found themselves caught in a web of conflicting interpretations; considered both pirates and patriots depending on the lens through which their actions are viewed. These figures, often respected as heroes in some regions, have been condemned as criminals in others.

| 37 | |

One figure about which people hold conflicting views is Francis Drake, a renowned English explorer and naval commander of the Elizabethan era. Celebrated as a national hero in England, Drake was regarded as a pirate by the Spanish Empire, England's enemy at the time. Drake's fearless raids on Spanish ships and coastal settlements, most notably those he carried out while travelling all the way around the globe aboard the *Golden Hind*, earned him fame and wealth in England. To the English, he embodied the spirit of adventure and of the expansion of England's influence overseas.

| 38 | |

However, despite the differing viewpoints, Drake's actions were often driven by the interests of his own nation, making it difficult to categorise him solely as a pirate or patriot. He carried out his raids on Spanish ships as part of a strategy to undermine Spanish dominance in the New World and ensure the prosperity and security of England. It is this complexity that fuels the debate surrounding his legacy, leaving us with a more complex understanding of his place in history.

| 39 | |

When the British threatened the port of New Orleans, Lafitte joined forces with the American military, providing crucial intelligence and leading a diverse group of private individuals to defend the city. His assistance was instrumental in pushing back against the British invasion, making him a hero in the eyes of many Americans. Lafitte's actions were seen as an act of patriotism, protecting American interests and preserving the young nation's sovereignty. Lafitte's actions were not only motivated by the desire to help others, though. By aiding the United States, he sought to secure his own privateering operations and protect his base of operations in Barataria, which had thrived under not very strict enforcement by Spanish authorities. Lafitte's actions exemplify the interaction between personal motivations and national interests that shape the perception of historical figures. The two sides of Lafitte's activities add a layer of complexity to his character and makes it less clear whether he was a pirate or patriot.

| 40 | |

Also known as Gráinne Mhaol, Grace O'Malley was a 16th-century Irish noblewoman who became a legendary figure for her seafaring exploits. Operating along the western coast of Ireland, O'Malley challenged English dominance and asserted her independence, making her a symbol of Irish resistance against English rule. Her raids on English ships and fortresses earned her a reputation as a pirate that should be feared. However, in Ireland, O'Malley was hailed a national hero and patriot, especially among the Gaelic families who saw her as a defender of Irish interests. Her resistance against the English crown and her diplomatic efforts to protect her family's lands in the face of colonial expansion made her popular amongst the Irish people.

| 41 | |

O'Malley's actions were deeply rooted in her commitment to the welfare and independence of her people. While her methods may have involved piracy, they were driven by a desire to resist colonialism and protect the interests of her homeland. This person's legacy as both a pirate and patriot highlights the complexity of historical figures and the way in which can combine heroic resistance and criminal activities.

| 42 | |

The narratives surrounding these international figures demonstrate the subjectivity of defining patriotism and piracy. Personal motivations, national interests and historical context all come together to create a more multi-dimensional understanding of these individuals' actions. The debate surrounding their legacies reflects the complex nature of history itself, where different interpretations emerge based on one's point of view.

| 43 | |

A Yet, from the perspective of the English, this person was a pirate who posed a threat to their control over Ireland. The English crown attempted to suppress the activities they were involved in and viewed them as a symbol of rebellion. The conflicting narratives surrounding this figure demonstrate how historical figures can be portrayed in contrasting lights, depending on the vantage point of the storyteller.

B However, their status as a patriot was not universally recognised. The Spanish, whose vessels this figure had often targeted, continued to view him as a pirate. The situation highlighted the complexities of labelling historical figures, as they could be both admired as heroic and despised as reckless, depending on the perspective of the observer.

C However, from the Spanish perspective, these actions constituted piracy and acts of aggression against their empire. The Spanish crown condemned him as a criminal and sought to bring him to justice. The conflict between Spain and England during this period further intensified the divisions. To the Spanish, this figure made very clear the dishonest nature of pirates and the threat they posed to their maritime dominance.

D The myths that have been created around Drake have led to him being seen as the perfect English gentleman. This is true to such an extent that few people today are even aware of the fact that he was essentially sent out by his Queen Gloriana to attack and steal from other ships. The aim of the English state at this point in the 16th century, and, indeed, into the 17th-century too, was state-sponsored theft as a means to gain an advantage over the country's international rivals for naval dominance. Seeing Drake in this light significantly alters our perceptions of his character.

E By exploring these stories, we are reminded that historical figures are not easily confined to simplistic labels. The tales of these pirates-turned-patriots or patriots-turned-pirates demonstrate the complex nature of their actions and the challenges inherent in crafting a definitive historical narrative. It is through embracing these complexities that we gain a deeper understanding of the past and the diverse perspectives that shape our understanding of history.

F The examples given here provide valuable insights into the challenges of categorising historical figures as either pirates or patriots. These individuals, celebrated as heroes by their supporters, were simultaneously condemned as criminals by opposing states. The complexity arises from the diverse perspectives shaped by political, cultural, and economic factors.

G Jean Lafitte, a French American pirate of the early 19th century, presents another fascinating example of the contrasting interpretations of his actions in a similar way to Drake. Lafitte operated in the Gulf of Mexico and the Caribbean, primarily targeting Spanish ships and disrupting their trade routes. While his activities would be considered piracy by most standards, Lafitte found favour with the United States during the War of 1812.

H The ambiguity lies in the diverse perspectives arising from contrasting political, cultural and economic interests. Here we take a closer look at the stories of three notable historical examples who were simultaneously celebrated as patriots by their supporters while being given the name of 'pirates' by rival states.

Cambridge C2 Proficiency Reading

Part 7

You are going to read an extract from a magazine article in which five judges give aspiring judges advice on how to achieve this career goal. For questions 44–53, choose from the sections (A–E). The sections may be selected more than once.

In which section are the following mentioned?

the importance of developing an understanding of people's needs and feelings	44
the need to keep up to date with changes in the field of law	45
the need to work hard while you are in compulsory education	46
the importance of not underestimating the burden of duty that judges bear	47
the importance of being highly rated in your academic studies	48
the importance of taking a higher degree at university	49
the importance of undertaking voluntary work	50
the need to undertake activities outside of your studies from a young age	51
the need to show that you are not biased or easily influenced	52
the need to remain intellectually curious	53

A Guide to Pursuing a Career as a Judge in the UK:
Nurturing the Aspiring Judges of Tomorrow

Five lawyers give advice to aspiring lawmakers on how they might become a judge.

A: Natalie Derry

As a senior judge, it is both my privilege and duty to provide you with invaluable advice, ethical considerations and an overview of the academic journey required to pursue this noble profession. Embrace the intellectual ability and moral compass necessary to uphold justice and make a lasting impact on society. During your educational journey, there are several key stages and considerations to bear in mind: you must be in no doubt that you will need to dedicate yourself to your academic studies at school from a young age, placing emphasis on subjects such as English, History, Law and the Social Sciences. Cultivate critical thinking, logical reasoning and effective communication skills through participation in debates and other non-academic activities.

B: Richard Canterbury

In preparation for university, select subjects aligned with your aspiration to become a judge, such as Law, History, Politics or Philosophy. You must achieve excellent grades in your final school examinations, as this will significantly contribute to the strength of your university applications. Seek opportunities to gain practical experience in the legal field through internships, shadowing judges or working with local law firms. For your undergraduate studies, enroll in a reputable university offering a qualifying law degree (LLB), one that is known for its academic reputation and strong faculty. Dedicate yourself to legal studies, exploring core modules such as Constitutional Law, Criminal Law and Legal Systems while also exploring specialised areas of interest. Actively participate in legal societies and debating competitions, and undertake unpaid work to help vulnerable people. This will help you to foster practical skills and build networks within the legal community. Strive to achieve a good grade in your first degree, as academic excellence is highly regarded in the judicial selection process.

C: Katy Lowe

Consider pursuing a postgraduate law degree, such as a Master of Law, to deepen your legal knowledge. You could specialise in areas such as Constitutional Law, International Law or Human Rights. Utilise this stage to undertake research projects, publish articles by contributing to legal journals to demonstrate your commitment to academic pursuits and intellectual growth. Additionally, networking events and conferences provide opportunities to foster connections with legal professionals, including professors, practitioners and judges. It is hard to overstate the importance of ethical and moral considerations. Judges are expected to have the strongest moral compass, and if you do become a judge your integrity and opinions will always be under the microscope. Embody and cultivate impartiality, ensuring that personal beliefs, biases or affiliations do not compromise your ability to deliver fair and just decisions. Uphold independence, maintaining a neutral stance while interpreting and applying the law, even in the face of societal or political pressures.

D: Archibald Lohner

Strictly follow the Code of Judicial Conduct, which encompasses principles of integrity and avoiding conflicts of interest. Display integrity in your personal and professional life, ensuring transparency, honesty and accountability in all your actions. Treat all individuals with respect and courtesy, regardless of their background, and be receptive to diverse perspectives while maintaining a strong commitment to equality before the law. You must embrace lifelong learning, staying up-to-date with legal developments, precedents and the evolving values of society. Participate in continuing education programmes, judicial training courses and professional conferences to enhance your knowledge and skills. As you embark on your journey towards becoming a judge, remember that the pursuit of justice requires dedication, integrity and a profound understanding of the law's complexities. Develop your intellectual capabilities, uphold the highest ethical standards and remain committed to the principles of independence. Strive to make a positive impact on society by ensuring that justice is served, and the rule of law is upheld. Embrace the opportunities available to you during your academic years, seize every chance to expand your knowledge and actively engage in activities that foster your understanding of the legal system and its intricate details.

E: Phyllis Sanbury

Remember that the path to becoming a judge is not solely about academic achievement. It requires personal growth, moral reflection and the development of a strong character. Treat every encounter and experience as an opportunity to enhance your empathy and respect for the diverse perspectives and backgrounds of the individuals who may come before you in court. I would recommend seeking out experienced judges and legal professionals who can guide you and give you advice throughout your career. These endeavours will contribute to your growth as a judge and enable you to make well-informed, fair and unbiased decisions that impact people's lives. As you set off on this noble path, remember that the role of a judge is one of immense responsibility and influence. The decisions you make will shape the lives of individuals and have a lasting impact on society as a whole. Approach each case with a profound sense of integrity, compassion and dedication to justice, always striving to ensure that your rulings reflect the highest ethical standards.

Cambridge C2 Proficiency Reading — Answer sheet

Name _____   Date _____

Part 5

Mark the appropriate answer.

0	A ☐	B ☐	C ■	D ☐
31	A ☐	B ☐	C ☐	D ☐
32	A ☐	B ☐	C ☐	D ☐
33	A ☐	B ☐	C ☐	D ☐
34	A ☐	B ☐	C ☐	D ☐
35	A ☐	B ☐	C ☐	D ☐
36	A ☐	B ☐	C ☐	D ☐

Part 6

Add the appropriate answer.

37	38	39	40	41	42	43

Part 7

Add the appropriate answer.

44	45
46	47
48	49
50	51
52	53

Cambridge C2 Proficiency Reading

Test 5

Part 5

You are going to read an extract from an article. For questions 31–36, mark the appropriate answer (A, B, C or D) that you think fits best according to the text.

The History of Coca-Cola: A Journey of Taste and Success

The Coca-Cola Company, a global soft drink giant, has a rich and fascinating history spanning more than a century. From its humble beginnings as a medicinal drink to its position as one of the most recognisable brands worldwide, Coca-Cola has become an integral part of popular culture.

The origins of Coca-Cola can be traced back to the year 1886 and Atlanta, Georgia, where pharmacist John S. Pemberton created a unique beverage. Pemberton's mixture was initially intended as a medicinal tonic. The drink was then known as 'Pemberton's French Wine Coca' and marketed as a remedy for health issues like headache and fatigue. However, with the introduction of prohibition laws in the USA, Pemberton had to modify his formula to remove the alcohol. This led to the birth of the iconic Coca-Cola, a carbonated soft drink that captured the imagination of the public. The turning point for Coca-Cola came in 1894 when Asa Griggs Candler acquired the rights to the company. Under Candler's leadership, Coca-Cola experienced rapid growth and expansion. To boost sales, Candler introduced innovative marketing strategies, such as offering vouchers for free Coke samples and distributing branded merchandise. These strategies not only increased consumer interest, they also established the Coca-Cola brand as a symbol of the American lifestyle.

The introduction of the curved glass bottle in 1915 marked another milestone in the company's history. Designed to make Coke bottles distinguishable even in the dark, this new bottle became an iconic symbol, helping to solidify its brand identity and prevent imitation by competitors.

The Coca-Cola Company's global expansion began in the early 20th century when the company began selling licenses to bottle its drinks to other companies. This new franchise system led to bottling franchises being established outside the United States. In 1906, Cuba became the first country to hold a Coca-Cola franchise, followed by Canada, Panama and Puerto Rico. By the 1920s, Coca-Cola had established a presence in Europe, Asia and South America to become one of the first truly global brands.

Nevertheless, the company faced challenges in certain regions due to political and cultural differences. During World War II, for instance, Coca-Cola's German operations were cut off from the parent company in the United States. Max Keith, the head of Coca-Cola's German branch, devised a new drink using available ingredients, which became known as Fanta. This innovation ensured the survival of Coca-Cola in Germany during the war and led to the creation of another successful drinks line.

Over the years, the Coca-Cola Company expanded its product portfolio to cater to evolving consumer preferences. In 1960, the company introduced Sprite, a lemon- and lime-flavoured soft drink that quickly gained popularity among a younger demographic. Later, other brands like Fanta, Minute Maid and PowerAde were added to the Coca-Cola family through strategic acquisitions.

In the 1980s, Coca-Cola faced intense competition from rival brand PepsiCo. In response, the company launched 'New Coke', a reformulated version of its famous drink. Yet the public's strong attachment to the original taste prompted a negative reaction, leading Coca-Cola to reintroduce the classic formula as 'Coca-Cola Classic'. This episode highlighted the power of consumer loyalty and the significance of preserving a brand's heritage.

Coca-Cola's impact extends beyond its drinks. The company has made substantial efforts to reduce its environmental footprint by focusing on water conservation, energy efficiency and recycling initiatives. It has also been actively involved in promoting sustainable sourcing of ingredients and packaging materials.

Coca-Cola's commitment to social responsibility has also been evident throughout its history. In the early 20th century, the company played a significant role in shaping the modern image of Santa Claus through its advertisements by portraying him as a jolly, red-suited figure enjoying a Coca-Cola. This iconic depiction of Santa Claus has become ingrained in popular culture. Furthermore, the company has actively engaged in charitable initiatives. The Coca-Cola Foundation, established in 1984, has contributed to numerous causes, including education, sustainability and community development. Through initiatives like the '5by20' programme, Coca-Cola has empowered millions of female entrepreneurs worldwide through the provision of business training and resources.

In more recent times, Coca-Cola has adapted to changing consumer preferences and market trends. Recognising the growing demand for healthier drinks options, the company has expanded its product range to include low-calorie and sugar-free alternatives. It has also introduced smaller portion sizes to promote moderation and launched a variety of flavoured water and tea products.

Test 5

31 Why did Pemberton change Coca-Cola's formula in its early years?

  A some people suffered from health problems after drinking it
  B because of a change to legislation affecting the drinks industry
  C its marketing materials made fraudulent claims about it
  D American customers did not like the European ingredients

32 What change in Coca-Cola's approach to business occurred under new leadership?

  A It gave away all of its beverages for free for a limited period of time.
  B It introduced a new bottle for its beverage which had an iconic shape.
  C It streamlined its production processes to increase its productivity.
  D It transmitted messages about its products to the public more proactively.

33 What played a decisive role in helping Coca-Cola establish a wider presence?

  A allowing external companies to pay for the right to package and sell its drink
  B taking the decision to put Coca-Cola on sale at retail outlets all over the world
  C the removal of trade barriers between North America and neighbouring countries
  D offering concessions to manufacturers in the Caribbean and Central America

34 What was the product of communication problems between branches of the company during World War II?

  A an upgrading of the quality of its drinks
  B an expansion of their product range
  C the establishment of European and North American divisions
  D innovations in technology

35 What lesson did Coca-Cola learn from introducing a new drink in the late 20th Century?

  A it shouldn't be too bound by its history of constantly innovating
  B it should not try to recreate its competitors' flavours
  C it didn't need to try so hard to compete with rival drinks manufacturers
  D its customers appreciate the unique taste of the brand's drinks

36 What recent change has Coca-Cola made in response to changing consumer preferences?

  A it has become involved in endeavours to promote greater equality
  B it pays closer attention to the nutritional value of its beverages
  C it has sought to position itself with key cultural events such as Christmas
  D it has reduced the number of drinks that it produces

Part 6

You are going to read an extract from a newspaper article. Seven paragraphs have been removed. Select from the paragraphs A–H the one that fits each gap (questions 37–43). There is one extra paragraph that you do not need to use.

The Evolution of Farming: Exploring Innovations in Agriculture

The agricultural sector has witnessed a remarkable transformation in recent years. In this article, we examine the benefits, challenges and implications of these innovations in terms of their contribution to the understanding of how technological advancements are revolutionising the agricultural landscape.

| 37 | |

Farming is clearly an essential component of human civilisation. Without farming we would not have adequate food supplies, and human life on Earth would struggle to survive. Yet farming has also experienced profound changes over centuries. The introduction of new technologies and scientific discoveries has significantly impacted agricultural practices, leading to increased efficiency, productivity and sustainability.

| 38 | |

Unmanned aerial vehicles, commonly known as drones, have gained prominence in various industries, including agriculture. Drones equipped with high-resolution cameras and sensors offer farmers the ability to monitor crop health, detect pest infestations and assess the general condition of their fields. Additionally, drones enable precise application of fertilisers and pesticides, reducing waste and improving resource management.

| 39 | |

Genetic modification has opened new avenues in crop improvement, offering enhanced resistance to pests, diseases and environmental stresses. GM foods, which involve the incorporation of desirable traits into crop plants, have shown promising results in increasing productivity and improving food quality. By employing biotechnology, farmers can cultivate crops that are more resistant to drought, require fewer chemical inputs and possess improved nutritional profiles. Nevertheless, the introduction of GM foods has generated debate and concern regarding their long-term effects on human health and the environment. Rigorous scientific assessments, comprehensive labelling systems and transparent communication are imperative to ensure consumer confidence and enable informed choices. Furthermore, regulatory frameworks need to be in place to address issues such as patent protection, intellectual property rights and potential ecological risks associated with the use of GM crops.

| 40 | |

Water scarcity and efficient water management pose significant challenges to agriculture. Automated irrigation systems offer a potential solution by enabling farmers to monitor soil moisture levels and apply water precisely when and where it is needed. These systems utilise sensors, weather data and sophisticated control mechanisms to optimise water usage, reduce runoff and prevent over-irrigation. By ensuring the efficient allocation of water resources, automated water systems contribute to water conservation and sustainability in farming.

| 41 | |

While the innovations discussed offer immense potential for transforming agriculture, several challenges and implications must be addressed for their successful implementation. Firstly, there is a need for comprehensive policies and regulations that guide the responsible adoption of these technologies. These policies should consider factors such as safety, privacy, environmental impact and social acceptance. Furthermore, public-awareness campaigns and education initiatives can help bridge the gap between farmers, consumers and policymakers, fostering informed decision-making and promoting dialogue.

| 42 | |

Additionally, ethical considerations surrounding the use of these technologies should be thoroughly evaluated. The potential impact on biodiversity, unintended consequences on ecosystems and the long-term effects on human health and well-being should be carefully monitored and assessed. Therefore, multi-disciplinary collaborations involving scientists, policymakers, farmers and consumers are crucial to dealing with the ethical implications of agricultural innovations.

| 43 | |

A   Farmers need access to reliable and accurate data, sophisticated machinery and specialised knowledge to effectively implement precision-farming practices. Additionally, issues related to data ownership, the ability to coordinate different items of machinery with each other and standardisation must be addressed to promote the widespread adoption of these techniques.

B   Several contributors, such as climate change and population growth, put ever-increasing demands on agriculture, particularly in developing nations, making the achievement of such aims more difficult, yet more important. Recent innovations such as drones, GM foods and automated irrigation have emerged as promising solutions to address the challenges faced by farmers in the modern era. Many of these innovations are fascinating and have the potential to revolutionise farming practices.

C   Agricultural innovation undoubtedly has many different aspects, but it also has the potential to revolutionise agriculture by increasing productivity, reducing environmental impact and promoting sustainable practices. However, their successful implementation requires careful planning, comprehensive policies and a complex understanding of the challenges and implications involved. Through responsible adoption and appropriate regulations, these innovations can empower farmers to meet the growing demand for food while reducing the environmental footprint of agriculture. As we try to understand the complexities of the modern farming landscape, it is essential to prioritise sustainability, inclusivity and ethical considerations to ensure a prosperous and resilient agricultural future.

D   Once confrontation has been replaced by cooperation between these various stakeholders, the digital divide then needs to be acknowledged and addressed. Access to technology and digital infrastructure varies across regions and communities, potentially creating inconsistencies in the adoption and benefits of these innovations. Efforts should be made to provide fair and equal access to technological resources, ensuring that small-scale farmers and marginalised communities can also make use of these advancements.

E   By providing real-time data and imagery, drones assist in making informed decisions about the necessary measures and amounts, which lead to improved yield and reduced operational costs. However, the integration of drones in farming is not without its challenges. Limited flight endurance, legal restrictions and the need for skilled operators are factors that must be addressed to make the most of their potential. Furthermore, concerns regarding privacy, data security and airspace regulations need to be carefully considered and managed to ensure responsible and ethical drone usage in agriculture.

F   An area that tends to be less complicated legally and ethically is that of precision farming, also known as site-specific farming or satellite farming, which involves the use of advanced technologies to optimise agricultural practices. Through the integration of data analytics, remote sensing and GPS technologies, precision farming enables farmers to adapt their activities to specific areas within their fields. This approach allows for precise nutrient application, irrigation management and planting strategies, thereby reducing waste and maximising crop yield. The adoption of precision-farming techniques, however, requires significant investments in infrastructure and data-management systems.

G   Drawing on extensive research and data evidence, we shall explore the potential of these innovations to enhance productivity, reduce environmental impact and promote sustainable farming practices. Furthermore, we will highlight the importance of comprehensive policies and awareness campaigns to ensure the responsible use of these technologies.

H   However, the implementation of such automated methods necessitates careful consideration of factors such as cost-effectiveness, compatibility with existing infrastructure and technical expertise. Farmers must assess the suitability of these systems for their specific farming conditions and evaluate the return on investment. Moreover, appropriate training and support should be provided to farmers to ensure proper installation, operation, and maintenance of these systems.

Part 7

You are going to read an extract from an article in which five actors describe their favourite character from William Shakespeare's plays. For questions 44–53, choose from the sections (A–E). The sections may be selected more than once.

In which section are the following mentioned?

a scene where a character is confronted by an uncomfortable truth	44
an appreciation of a character's contradiction of society's expectations of them	45
still having to work hard to portray a character despite having done it many times	46
an appreciation of how their character can behave in many different ways	47
the significant change in the personality and behaviour of a character	48
how a Shakespearean character can go beyond conventional gender boundaries	49
finding a way to access what is going on in the mind of their character	50
the linguistic complexities of a character's speeches	51
the amusing back-and-forth between their character and another character	52
how their character experiences remorse	53

My favourite Shakespearean role

Five actors who are very experienced at playing characters from the plays of Shakespeare explain their favourite role to play

A: Sir Alan Wallace as Macbeth

As an experienced actor with a profound appreciation for the works of William Shakespeare, my favourite role to date has been Macbeth. Portraying the ambitious and troubled Scottish general allowed me to explore the complexities of human nature. I relished the challenge of capturing Macbeth's transformation from a brave and noble warrior to a ruthless tyrant dealing with feelings of guilt. Shakespeare's language provides some great material for an actor, and Macbeth's speeches are particularly captivating. The famous 'Tomorrow, and tomorrow, and tomorrow' speech encompasses the despair and hopelessness that Macbeth experiences. It's a moment where the character's vulnerability is clear to everyone, and, as an actor, I strive to convey the raw emotions embedded within the words. The role continues to challenge and inspire me, allowing me to explore the depths of human nature through the lens of Shakespeare's genius.

B: Dame Julie Dear as Lady Macbeth

Lady Macbeth always has a special place in my heart. This powerful and extremely complex character has been a source of endless fascination throughout my career. Portraying her journey from a manipulative and ambitious woman to a tormented soul consumed by guilt is a true acting challenge. Lady Macbeth's speech in Act 1, Scene 5, where she calls upon the spirits to fill her with cruelty, demonstrates her strong will and burning desire for power. Exploring the depths of her mind, I aim to convey her internal struggles and the tragic consequences of her actions. What I find most intriguing about Lady Macbeth is her status as a woman in a male-dominated world. Through her character, Shakespeare provides a fascinating exploration of femininity and the destructive forces that can arise when ambition is out of control.

C: Ian Stewart as King Lear

In my award-winning career, one Shakespearean role stands out above all others, and that is the tragic figure of King Lear. This complex character exhibits the full range of human emotions. One of the most powerful scenes in the play occurs during the storm on the heath, where Lear confronts the harsh realities of his own stupidity. The raw vulnerability and emotional turmoil of this moment provide an immense challenge for any actor. It is a scene where the full force of Lear's internal struggle becomes apparent, and I strive to convey his pain and anguish with utmost sincerity. King Lear offers a profound examination of human nature, exposing the fragility that can consume even the mightiest of individuals. The poetic richness of his speeches, particularly during the emotional moments of self-reflection, gives me the opportunity to connect with the audience on a deeper level. It is a great challenge, but also a privilege to bring such a complex character to life.

D: Kevin Woods as Hamlet

Ah, the world-famous Prince of Denmark, Hamlet! It is with great enthusiasm that I declare this Shakespearean role to be my absolute favourite. The complexities of Hamlet's character, his philosophical reflections and his quest for justice provide a treasure trove for any actor. Hamlet's speech in Act III, Scene I, where he considers the nature of existence with the iconic phrase 'To be, or not to be', remains one of the most renowned passages in all of literature. It is a moment of reflection that demonstrates the depth of Hamlet's psyche. Bringing this extensive inner life to the stage is a challenge I really enjoy. What sets Hamlet apart is his multi-dimensionality. He is simultaneously a scholar, a philosopher, a son seeking revenge and a prince caught in the web of political intrigue. Examining all of these layers and portraying the intricate emotions of a character trying to come to terms with life's most profound questions is an exhilarating journey for an actor.

E: Dame Mary Small as Beatrice in 'Much Ado About Nothing'

When it comes to Shakespearean roles, I am extremely fond of the quick-witted and spirited Beatrice from 'Much Ado About Nothing'. Portraying this fiercely independent and fiery character has been a true delight throughout my career. Beatrice's sharp wit and her ability to hold her own in a world dominated by men make her a timeless and empowering figure. She is a woman unafraid to speak her mind and challenge norms and expectations in society. It is a joy to bring her vibrant energy and dark humour to the stage. Shakespeare's language in 'Much Ado About Nothing' is particularly playful and filled with witty exchanges. The dialogue between Beatrice and Benedick is a delight to perform, as they shoot comments at each other, like two tennis players passing a ball. Portraying Beatrice also allows me to celebrate the strength and intelligence of women while also reminding audiences of the power of love and the importance of embracing vulnerability.

Cambridge C2 Proficiency Reading

Answer sheet

Name _____   Date _____

Part 5
Mark the appropriate answer.

| 0 | A ☐ | B ☐ | C ■ | D ☐ |

31	A ☐	B ☐	C ☐	D ☐
32	A ☐	B ☐	C ☐	D ☐
33	A ☐	B ☐	C ☐	D ☐
34	A ☐	B ☐	C ☐	D ☐
35	A ☐	B ☐	C ☐	D ☐
36	A ☐	B ☐	C ☐	D ☐

Part 6
Add the appropriate answer.

| 37 | 38 | 39 | 40 | 41 | 42 | 43 |

Part 7
Add the appropriate answer.

44	45
46	47
48	49
50	51
52	53

Cambridge
C2 Proficiency
Reading

Test 6

Part 5

You are going to read an extract from an article. For questions 31–36, mark the appropriate answer (A, B, C or D) that you think fits best according to the text.

Martin Corr Moves to The Big Smoke

"If you really want to do it, set a date that allows for ample planning and just do it." That was the advice I received from a friend, yet I do not think he was expecting me to make such a huge change. I've always been a dreamer. I've always wanted to be an actor, and from a young age I had been attracted by the prospect of the big city. Growing up in a small village, I would spend my time daydreaming about the lights and excitement of faraway places. My heart was set on London – a fascinating city of dreams that happened to be relatively close to me and where fame and fortune awaited those with enough determination.

I'd never been on such a long train ride, but the journey passed in what seemed like a few short minutes. Arriving in London, I was struck by the sheer magnitude of the city. Skyscrapers towered above me and the streets buzzed with energy. It was both exhilarating and overwhelming. With wide-eyed wonder, I began to explore the city, eager to make my mark.

Days turned into weeks, and I discovered, unfortunately, that the path to fame and fortune was not as straightforward as I had imagined. The initial thrill of being in London soon started to wear off and reality began to set in. My flatmates weren't very sociable. In fact, they weren't very nice to me at all. I imagined it was just because I was the last one to move in, but I always felt like an outsider. And the flat was really run-down and cold.

I attended countless auditions and got some work, only to be told that the performances were no longer going ahead at the last minute. Doubt began to creep into my mind, but I refused to give up. I knew that success required perseverance and resilience. One evening, while walking through Covent Garden, I stumbled upon a street performer who was throwing around batons of fire – juggling, in other words – while doing backflips, captivating the crowd with his skill. People were throwing coins and notes into his upturned cap. I stood at the edge of the crowd, completely amazed by the spectacle. As the show came to an end, I approached the performer, my heart pounding with excitement. I had done gymnastics for years when I was younger, and I thought I could probably learn a few of the tricks I had just witnessed. "Excuse me, sir," I said, my voice trembling. "I want to be like you – a performer. Can you teach me?" The street performer smiled kindly and agreed to mentor me!

Over the following weeks, I learned everything I could about the art of street performance. I learned to juggle and even to perform magic tricks. The streets became my stage, and over time I developed my skills, attracting larger and larger crowds each day. That sort of performing can bring a healthy income, albeit mostly in coins, but I didn't mind. It felt liberating to earn money in such a non-conventional manner, but most importantly I had managed to find a way to pay my rent.

One afternoon, as I was entertaining a particularly enthusiastic audience in my second month of shows, I caught the eye of a talent agent. He later told me he was intrigued by my 'charisma' and talent as a performer. The scout approached me right after the show.

"I think you have what it takes to make it big," he said, a glint of excitement in his eyes. "I don't suppose you act, do you?" I couldn't believe my ears!

"I'm a talent agent, and I believe I can help you reach the next level. How would you like to perform in front of a national audience?"

Overwhelmed with joy, I accepted the opportunity without hesitation. With the advice and support of the talent agent, I secured a spot on a popular television talent show. I remember feeling that the bright lights of the studio engulfed me as I stepped onto the stage, and my heart raced with excitement and anticipation.

Even if I do say so myself, my performance was sensational. The audience erupted in applause, and the judges were left in awe. From that moment on, my life changed forever. Offers poured in from all directions – movie roles, endorsements and even record deals. I had finally found the fame and fortune I had always dreamed of.

But amidst the glitz and glamour, I have never forgotten my humble beginnings. I still call my mum every night before she goes to bed, and I have used my success to inspire others. I returned to my small village, sharing my story with aspiring performers and encouraging them to follow their dreams.

Test 6

31 What made Martin want to move to London?

   A he thought it was an extremely interesting place

   B his friend suggested that he give it a try

   C the city's location in relation to the village where he grew up

   D he thought it would be easier to achieve his dreams there

32 Martin's first weeks in London are best characterised as being

   A full of exhilaration that quickly changed to disillusionment.

   B an exciting experience despite the loneliness he experienced.

   C full of frustration due to the difficulties he experienced on many fronts.

   D an energising experience which spurred him on to achieve his dreams.

33 How does Martin account for his change in artistic direction?

   A his lack of success in obtaining acting roles

   B his fascination with a performance he saw

   C the skills he had developed when he was young

   D the financial remuneration he could receive

34 It is suggested that Martin stood out as a street performer because he

   A performed in a way that nobody had experienced before.

   B had clearly gained a lot of experience as a performer.

   C had qualities as a performer that not everyone has.

   D was attracting large crowds to his performances.

35 Martin's career can be characterised as

   A a meteoric rise to fame under the guidance of someone with more experience.

   B a slow and gradual process that was accelerated by a lucky break.

   C a successful journey that would not have been possible without an industry insider.

   D a process that was decisively propelled forward by the support of the public on the streets.

36 The impression Martin gives is that

   A he is solely focused on helping other performers now.

   B he hasn't succumbed to the negative effects of fame.

   C he now dislikes the bright lights of the big city.

   D he is somewhat disillusioned with performing now.

Part 6

You are going to read an extract from a magazine article. Seven paragraphs have been removed. Select from the paragraphs A–H the one that fits each gap (questions 37–43). There is one extra paragraph that you do not need to use.

Man's Lost Cousins: Unveiling the Enigmatic World of Prehistoric Humans

It is not unusual to hear Prehistoric humans being commonly referred to as man's lost cousins: our own evolution can be traced back to these earlier beings. Here we provide an overview of the evolutionary history, anatomical characteristics and cultural significance of this extinct human-like species. We aim to shed light on the fascinating story of our ancestry as humans.

| 37 | |

In a very significant paper published in 2002, Wood and Richmond explored the evolutionary relationship between humans and our extinct cousins. The researchers argued that the human line of descent took a different path from the common ancestor shared with chimpanzees around six-to-seven million years ago. This change ultimately led to the emergence of multiple human species, each with unique anatomical and behavioural characteristics.

| 38 | |

In recent years, anthropologists working in this field have increasingly focused on understanding the cultural practices of prehistoric humans. A ground-breaking study by d'Errico (2012) investigated the symbolic behaviour of Neanderthals, a species closely related to *Homo sapiens*. The researchers analysed engraved objects from several archaeological sites and proposed that Neanderthals possessed the capacity for symbolic thought and expression, further highlighting the link between our species and our extinct relatives.

| 39 | |

The Denisovans, another enigmatic prehistoric human species, were first identified through ancient DNA analysis in 2010. A study by Reich (2011) demonstrated that Denisovans contributed genetic material to present-day populations in the Pacific Ocean. The scale of their movement that this discovery represents serves to highlight the complex interactions between different groups of humans.

| 40 | |

Through an exploration of various research papers, we have dived into the captivating world of prehistoric humans. These ancient relatives have left an indelible mark on our understanding of human evolution and our place in the natural world. Researchers have analysed the evolutionary history, anatomical characteristics and cultural significance of prehistoric humans, and have been able to put together a compelling narrative of our ancestral line. The diverse range of species, such as *Australopithecus sediba*, Neanderthals and the Denisovans, challenge our preconceived notions of a linear progression and highlight the intricate web of human evolution.

| 41 | |

The cultural significance of prehistoric humans has also come to the forefront in recent years. The study by d'Errico (2012) demonstrated that Neanderthals engaged in symbolic behaviour, challenging previous assumptions about their cognitive abilities. This finding further highlights the need to remove any clear dividing line between our species and our extinct cousins.

| 42 | |

Understanding the environmental context in which prehistoric humans lived is crucial to deciphering their adaptations and lifestyles. The study by Groucutt (2018) shed light on the co-existence of *Homo sapiens* with other prehistoric humans, such as Neanderthals, in the Arabian Peninsula during the Late Pleistocene. Such findings provide a glimpse into the dynamic nature of human evolution and the complexities of interactions between different species of prehistoric humans.

| 43 | |

A   Research papers by Wood and Richmond (2002) have revealed that the separation that occurred between humans and chimpanzees took place approximately six or seven million years ago, leading to the evolution of these multiple human species. The picture of one of these called *Australopithecus sediba* has underscored the complexity of our ancestral tree.

B   The study of such prehistoric humans is an exciting and evolving field of research that offers valuable insights into our evolutionary past. Over the years, numerous scientific publications have contributed to expanding our knowledge and understanding of these fascinating creatures. This article seeks to provide an overview of the key findings from selected research papers, illuminating the diversity, adaptations, and evolutionary paths of prehistoric humans.

C   Indeed, the discovery of ancient DNA has revolutionised our understanding of the genetic interactions between early humans and prehistoric humans. In a landmark paper published in 2010, Professor Richard Green analysed the DNA of a Neanderthal individual. The study revealed that modern humans of non-African descent share a small percentage of genetic material with Neanderthals, suggesting interbreeding between the two species.

D   As research continues to uncover new fossils, refine dating techniques and utilise advanced genomic analyses, our understanding of prehistoric humans will undoubtedly continue to evolve. The captivating story of our lost cousins serves as a constant reminder of the rich tapestry of human evolution and our inter-connectedness with the natural world.

E   Furthermore, genetic studies, particularly those by Green (2010) and Reich (2011), have revealed fascinating insights into the genetic legacy of prehistoric humans that we also still experience the impact of today. The discovery that modern humans share a small percentage of genetic material with Neanderthals and Denisovans suggests intricate interactions and gene flow between these different prehistoric human groups.

F   To understand the ecological adaptations and lifestyles of prehistoric humans, researchers have sought to reconstruct the paleoenvironmental contexts in which these species thrived. Research undertaken by Groucutt (2018) examined fossil and archaeological evidence from the Arabian Peninsula, shedding light on the dispersal of *Homo sapiens* and our interactions with other humans during the Late Pleistocene period (about 2.6 million years ago to 11,700 years ago). The findings indicated that our species coexisted with other prehistoric humans, including Neanderthals, in this region, offering glimpses into the dynamic nature of human evolution.

G   It would be a mistake to assume that prehistoric humans lived stationary lives as the evidence suggests that they could be extremely mobile. Beginning from approximately two million years ago, prehistoric humans began to move out of Africa and into other parts of the world. This initial migration was followed by those of other archaic humans that lived around 500,000 years ago and who are likely to have been the ancestors of Denisovans and Neanderthals as well as modern humans. Early prehistoric humans seem to have been crossing land bridges that have now sunk and been erased from human geography.

H   This former species demonstrates that some prehistoric humans possessed both ape-like and human-like characteristics. Comprehensive study of it has been carried out after fossil remains of examples of the species were discovered in South Africa. The mosaic-like combination of different traits challenged the previously held notion of a linear evolutionary progression and highlighted the complexity of prehistoric human evolution.

Part 7

You are going to read an extract from an article in which five people involved in the staging of live concerts share insights into their work. For questions 44–53, choose from the sections (A–E). The sections may be selected more than once.

In which section are the following mentioned?

the different treatment that artists and crew receive	44
determining likely levels of interest in the shows amongst the public	45
the business deals that take place so a concert can be staged in a specific location	46
the balancing of income and outgoings	47
the considerations involved in planning shows	48
how artists publicise their shows	49
the potentially fatal consequences of inadequate preparations	50
the importance of liaising with local authorities	51
the need to follow specifications	52
the need to coordinate the location of concerts effectively	53

The Logistics of a Stadium World Tour

A

Embarking on a stadium world tour is a colossal undertaking that requires meticulous planning, coordination and resources. Major bands such as the Rolling Stones and Guns N' Roses have astounded audiences across the globe with their awe-inspiring performances, and, behind the scenes, an intricate web of logistics supports the realisation of these monumental spectacles. A tour involves months of planning before it even starts, mountains of bureaucracy at every turn and thousands of team members working together to make the tour a reality. A stadium world tour typically spans several months to accommodate numerous cities and countries. Bands like the afore-mentioned Rolling Stones or Guns N' Roses plan their tours carefully, considering factors such as geographic location, transportation logistics and venue availability. Zig-zag movement across a continent, for instance, must be avoided as it is inconvenient and costly. The process often commences a year or more in advance to ensure adequate preparation and organisation.

B

The first stage of organising a stadium world tour involves identifying potential tour dates and the tour route. Bands collaborate with their management teams, promoters and booking agents to determine the regions and cities that they should aim to visit. Factors like market demand, fan base and historical ticket-sales data help in shaping the tour itinerary. The selection of stadiums is a critical component of a successful world tour, as stadiums offer vast seating capacities, enabling bands to cater to large audiences. Popular venues include iconic stadiums like Wembley Stadium in London, Madison Square Garden in New York or the Maracanã Stadium in Rio de Janeiro. Negotiations with venue management involve securing dates, contract agreements and analysing the infrastructure to ensure it can accommodate the band's production requirements.

C

Stadium tours demand extensive technical infrastructure to deliver the electrifying performances that fans anticipate. Bands work closely with production companies specialising in live events to design and execute these intricate setups. The technical team collaborates with the band's crew to ensure the integration of the show elements. Failures in these areas can have grave consequences. AC/DC's 'Razors Edge' world tour experienced a devastating incident in Salt Lake City, Utah, where a combination of poor planning and a tragic accident led to the deaths of three fans. The band's elaborate stage design included a central structure resembling a large cannon. During the performance of their song 'For Those About to Rock', a firework exploded prematurely, engulfing the stage in flames. The explosion caused panic among the audience, resulting in a stampede towards the exits. The incident prompted a thorough re-evaluation of safety protocols and practices in the live music industry, emphasising the vital need for meticulous planning, rigorous safety checks and effective communication to prevent such tragic accidents.

D

A stadium world tour involves moving an enormous amount of equipment, personnel and artists from one location to another. Bands typically travel in a private jet or a fleet of chartered planes to ensure efficiency and comfort. The crew and equipment, meanwhile, are transported via a fleet of trucks, which may number anywhere from 10 to 30, depending on the scale of the production. It's estimated that a crew of 150-to-200 people is required to run a stadium world tour smoothly. The logistics team plays a pivotal role in the success of a stadium tour. They manage accommodation, catering, ground transportation, visas and work permits for the entire crew. Each tour stop involves a meticulously planned schedule, ensuring smooth 'load-ins' and 'load-outs', soundchecks, rehearsals and media engagements. The team also coordinates with local police, airport authorities and venue staff. Promotion and ticketing are essential elements for a successful stadium world tour. Bands work closely with marketing teams and promoters to generate buzz and awareness through traditional and digital channels. Tickets are typically sold through various platforms, including ticketing websites and authorised resellers. For a high-demand tour, ticket sales can reach hundreds of thousands, generating significant revenue.

E

A stadium world tour involves substantial costs, but it also presents lucrative opportunities for bands. The major expenses include production costs, crew salaries, transportation, accommodation, venue fees and promotional activities. The costs can vary significantly depending on the band's requirements, the number of tour dates and the scale of the production. On average, a stadium world tour can cost tens of millions of dollars. Revenue generation primarily comes from ticket sales, which can reach astronomical figures given the capacity of stadiums. Additional sources of revenue include merchandise sales, sponsorship deals and licensing agreements. Bands may also explore partnerships with streaming platforms or television networks to broadcast live performances, further expanding their revenue potential. With large crowds and high-profile events, security is of paramount importance. Bands employ teams of experienced security personnel to ensure the safety of the audience, crew and artists. Close collaboration with local law enforcement and venue security staff is crucial in implementing comprehensive security measures, including bag checks, metal detectors and crowd-control strategies. In recent years, there has been a growing emphasis on sustainability and reducing the environmental impact of stadium tours. Bands are increasingly incorporating eco-friendly practices into their tours, such as using renewable energy sources for power, implementing waste-management and recycling system, and promoting carbon-offset initiatives.

Cambridge C2 Proficiency Reading — Answer sheet

Name 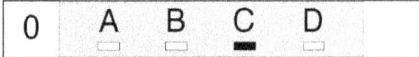 Date _____

Part 5
Mark the appropriate answer.

0	A ☐	B ☐	C ■	D ☐
31	A ☐	B ☐	C ☐	D ☐
32	A ☐	B ☐	C ☐	D ☐
33	A ☐	B ☐	C ☐	D ☐
34	A ☐	B ☐	C ☐	D ☐
35	A ☐	B ☐	C ☐	D ☐
36	A ☐	B ☐	C ☐	D ☐

Part 6
Add the appropriate answer.

37	38	39	40	41	42	43

Part 7
Add the appropriate answer.

44	45
46	47
48	49
50	51
52	53

Cambridge C2 Proficiency Reading

Test 7

Part 5

You are going to read an extract from an article. For questions 31–36, mark the appropriate answer (A, B, C or D) that you think fits best according to the text.

Jeff Buckley

In the realm of musical brilliance, several artists stand out as guiding lights. Having left an indelible mark on the cosmos of sound, Jeff Buckley is undoubtedly amongst such illustrious company. Born to renowned musician Tim Buckley and his then-partner, Mary Guibert, Jeff emerged from a family steeped in talent and artistry. During his early life, he absorbed the sounds of his father and explored his own artistic path.

Buckley's journey as a guitarist was shaped by diverse influences. His father's experimental folk-rock style clearly left a lasting impression on him as he received so much exposure to it in his formative years. Guitar virtuosos such as Jimi Hendrix and Jimmy Page inspired his own exploration of the instrument and had the advantage of being somewhat set apart from his home environment. As a direct result of these influences, Buckley developed a unique approach to guitar playing which appealed to that blended delicate fingerpicking with bursts of raw intensity – like nothing ever heard before. His sound came to be seen as a cosmic dance due to its lucid qualities and heavenly sound. It resonated with both a fragile beauty and earthbound passion.

A significant turning point in Jeff Buckley's life came when he moved to New York City in the early 1990s. Buckley was in his early twenties at that point and had just started to establish himself as a musician in his own right. Once in New York, he forged connections with other successful musicians and began to further develop his own musical identity that appealed to music executives. It was during this time that he caught the attention of legendary record executive Steve Berkowitz, who signed Buckley to Columbia Records. The deal set the stage for his meteoric rise to musical fame and the creation of his most significant album 'Grace'.

Throughout his career, Jeff Buckley's impact on his peers was immeasurable. Fellow artists recognised his unparalleled talent and his ability to create music that touched the depths of the people's souls from very early on. Thom Yorke of Radiohead once remarked, "Jeff Buckley was an extraordinary musician and a truly gifted songwriter. His work had a profound influence on me, and I know he inspired countless others as well." Chris Martin of Coldplay echoed these sentiments, saying, "Jeff Buckley's music was like a revelation … his artistry pushed the boundaries of what was possible."

Tragically, Jeff Buckley's life was cut short in 1997 at the age of 30, but he left behind a legacy that continues to resonate to this day. His album 'Grace', released in 1994, remains a testament to his immense talent and artistic vision. Its haunting beauty and emotional depth have captivated audiences, going beyond genre and generations. *Rolling Stone* magazine hailed it as one of the greatest albums of all time, thus helping to solidify Buckley's place in the hall of fame of musical icons. Unfortunately, we will never know what music Buckley would have gone on to make had he lived longer, but all the indications are that he had not yet reached the peak of his musical powers.

Beyond his own music, Jeff Buckley's influence on subsequent generations of musicians, especially young aspiring musicians, cannot be overstated. His artistry has been a guiding light for countless artists who seek to channel vulnerability and raw, unfiltered feelings into their own creations. His voice and guitar playing continue to inspire awe and reverence after his death, serving as a constant reminder of the power of music to connect with the deepest corners of the human spirit. In the words of Bob Dylan, "Jeff Buckley was a pure drop in an ocean of noise. His voice was perfect, his guitar playing was incredible and his songs were like poetry. He was a true artist, and his impact will be felt for generations to come."

Jeff Buckley's music has a kind of other-worldly quality to it, as if he had been more than a mere mortal somehow. His early life led him on a journey of self-discovery. His meetings with music industry leaders and his signing to Columbia Records brought him to the attention of the mainstream. And while his life was tragically cut short, his legacy as an artist of extraordinary talent and emotional depth endures to this day. Jeff Buckley's stirring melodies continue to illuminate the night sky of the music world, a reminder of the power of artistry to touch our souls and elevate us to celestial heights.

31 It is suggested that the fact that Jeff Buckley's father was a musician

    A had the most significant influence on his early years as a musician.

    B was not as great an influence as the music of bigger stars who he listened to.

    C was an important influence, but not solely responsible for his style of playing.

    D made him react against the type of music his father played and go in a different direction.

32 How does the writer assess the impact of Buckley's move to New York on his career?

    A it helped him to establish a sound that the music industry found attractive

    B it enabled him to seek out opportunities to work with successful musicians

    C it opened his eyes to a much wider spectrum of musical styles

    D it gave him a taste for attention that helped to propel him to fame

33 According to the writer, Buckley's peers agree that he

    A was a more talented singer than any of his contemporaries.

    B was an innovator who had a big impact on them.

    C used conventional methods but still had a fresh sound.

    D was not appreciated enough by the public during his life.

34 It is suggested that if Buckley hadn't died prematurely, he would have

    A created songs with deeper meaning and more emotion.

    B continued in the same way musically.

    C taken a break from the spotlight after having reached his peak.

    D gone on to make even better music.

35 According to the writer, Buckley's influence has endured due to

    A his representation of a common spirit of youth.

    B his commitment to music in its purest form.

    C his technical skill and emotional honesty.

    D the many unique qualities of his voice.

36 The writer's overall impression is that Buckley

    A was able to tap into something that everyone can relate to.

    B seems to have been more than just a man with a guitar.

    C gave the public something they had been yearning for.

    D aspired to be viewed as something beyond just being a musician.

Part 6

You are going to read an extract from a newspaper article. Seven paragraphs have been removed. Select from the paragraphs A–H the one that fits each gap (questions 37–43). There is one extra paragraph that you do not need to use.

Fight for Your Rights: The Surge of Demonstrations in City Centres

In recent times, the urban landscape has become a battleground for those on the sidelines of society and the disenchanted, as citizens rise up in fervent opposition to oppressive systems. The streets of city centres have transformed into arenas where the voice of the people can be heard. These voices are demanding justice, equality and a better world. This surge in demonstrations is a testament to the indomitable spirit of those fighting for their rights and the recognition of their collective power.

37

The protest gained substantial support from various sectors of society, drawing attention to the systemic flaws that impede the realisation of equal educational opportunities. Public opinion polls indicated a clear majority in favour of the protesters' demands, reflecting a widespread recognition of the urgent need for reform. Media outlets largely offered a platform for demonstrators to voice their grievances, amplifying their concerns and generating public discourse.

38

Another demonstration that reverberated through the streets was the 'Climate Justice March' held in London. Fuelled by the undeniable reality of climate change and the urgent need for environmental action, people from all walks of life congregated to demand transformative policies to combat the ecological crisis. Banners adorned with phrases like 'Our Planet, Our Responsibility' and 'The Time for Change is Now' filled the skyline, capturing the essence of the protesters' demands.

39

The government's response to the Climate Justice march was a reflection of their entrenched interests in maintaining the status quo. Despite pretending to be concerned about environmental matters, the policy actions taken were woefully inadequate. This lack of meaningful action fuelled frustration among the demonstrators, who saw their government's response as a betrayal of their collective future. Nonetheless, the movement persisted, engaging in acts of civil disobedience and creating international solidarity to exert pressure on the authorities.

40

However, the response from the government and corporate entities was far from supportive. While some politicians offered rhetorical gestures in favour of workers' rights, real policy changes remained elusive. Corporations, concerned primarily with maximising profits, resisted the demands put forth by the protesters, often resorting to tactics aimed at undermining collective bargaining efforts.

41

The three demonstrations mentioned above are symbolic of a larger global trend that goes beyond geographical boundaries. They reflect the deep-seated discontent present below the surface within societies, caused by economic disparities, environmental degradation and systemic inequalities. The increasing frequency and scale of these demonstrations signal a collective awakening, as citizens recognise the power of unity and activism.

42

However, the responses from the authorities have been far from satisfactory. Governments and corporate entities have displayed a remarkable resistance to meaningful change, resorting to empty rhetoric and token gestures. This difference between the demands of the people and the actions of those in power has only served to increase the determination of the demonstrators, as they recognise that the fight for their rights is far from over.

43

A While political figures acknowledged the importance of education and the need for change, concrete policy actions remained elusive. The government's tepid response was not appropriate for the urgency of the situation, leading to continued discontent among the demonstrators. As the protest continued, tensions escalated, with some clashes erupting between the police and protesters. Despite the authorities' attempts to silence dissent, the 'Education for All' movement persisted, building support and gaining international attention.

B Due to the power of technology, however, it is now also possible for people to engage in acts of civil disobedience online. One example of this could be, for instance, filming protests or acts of brutality perpetuated by the police against protestors and then posting these on social media to ensure that the word gets out. The results of this could be to raise awareness of the protest, thus inspiring more people to take part in it or to collect and share evidence of protestors being mistreated. This could then be used to make a case against the police.

C Let us cast our gaze upon one such example of these kinds of collective struggles: 'Education for All' protest that unfolded in the heart of New York City. Tens of thousands of students, teachers and parents took to the streets, brandishing placards with slogans such as 'Equal Opportunities, Equal Minds' and 'Knowledge Knows No Boundaries'. The demonstration sought to challenge the educational inequalities deeply engrained in the system, which perpetuated social disparities and hindered upward mobility.

D Now we turn our attention to the 'Workers' Rights Rally', which was, in contrast, more of an inward-looking movement. It unfolded in the bustling streets of Paris. Thousands of workers, both unionised and non-unionised, congregated to demand fair wages, better working conditions and the right to collective bargaining. Signs proclaiming, 'No Justice, No Labour' and 'United We Stand' summed up the spirit of the protest, as workers from diverse sectors joined forces to confront the deep-rooted inequalities plaguing the labour market.

E These ongoing demonstrations also highlight the tension and conflict that arise when power structures are challenged. The clashes between protesters and law enforcement serve as a stark reminder of the struggles faced by those seeking justice and equality. Yet, in the face of adversity, these movements persist, drawing strength from their collective will to effect transformative change.

F This insubordination led to heightened tensions on the streets of Paris. Workers faced an intensified police presence, which sought to stifle the voices of dissent and maintain the status quo. In response, the rally took on a more militant character, with some clashes erupting between the demonstrators and law enforcement. This heightened level of confrontation highlighted the severity of the issues at hand and the determination of the workers to fight for their rights.

G This demonstration received a mixed response from the public and the media. While there were those who dismissed the protesters as idealistic and radical, a growing segment of society recognised the gravity of the climate emergency and stood in solidarity with the cause. Supportive voices in the media provided a platform for environmental activists to articulate their demands, highlighting the interconnectedness of climate justice with social and economic justice.

H What distinguishes these demonstrations is the ability of the protesters to use the power of public opinion and media attention. By articulating their demands through creative slogans, eye-catching banners and engaging storytelling, they have successfully generated discourse and help to build support. Social media platforms have played a crucial role in amplifying their messages, making it easier for information and media to be shared widely and easily.

Part 7

You are going to read an extract from an article in which five genealogists talk about their family history. For questions 44–53, choose from the sections (A–E). The sections may be selected more than once.

In which section are the following mentioned?

a family story that was deliberately kept under wraps	44
an ancestor who achieved international fame	45
an ancestor who helped to expand people's knowledge	46
actions of an ancestor that were powered by strong emotions	47
the feeling of being transported to a specific place	48
a new sense of belonging to a specific culture	49
surprise that an ancestor's character traits had not resurfaced	50
an ancestor who shared an interest that the writer already had	51
a discovery that led the writer to appreciate something more	52
a discovery that evokes images of luxury	53

Where do you think you came from?

Five amateur genealogists talk about a family secret they uncovered in their research.

A: The murderer

During my deep dive into the family archives, I unearthed a bone-chilling secret that left me trembling. Plain to see amongst layers of faded photographs and forgotten letters left in suitcase in my grandma's bedroom, I stumbled upon evidence that my great-great-grandfather was a cold-blooded murderer. As the truth unravelled before me, I pieced together a horrifying tale of betrayal and deceit. The newspapers of the time chronicled the heinous crime, which shocked the small community where my ancestors once resided. The details were gruesome, revealing a man driven by jealousy and vengeance. It appeared that my ancestor, plagued by envy, had ruthlessly taken the life of his business partner in a fit of rage. Though he managed to evade justice and live out his days in the shadows, the darkness of his crime tainted the family legacy. As I grapple with this revelation, I can't help but wonder how such a malevolent streak could be concealed within the depths of our family history.

B: The famous ballerina

Intriguingly, my genealogical expedition uncovered an enchanting hidden secret: my great-grandmother was a world-renowned ballerina. I stumbled upon her name delicately etched in faded posters and newspaper clippings, testament to her grace and mastery of the art. Her enchanting performances had captivated audiences on grand stages across the globe. Critics hailed her as a visionary, with a talent that went beyond the boundaries of traditional ballet. She embraced the stage with poise and elegance, her movements had a magical quality that left spectators spellbound. My heart swells with pride as I learn more about her extraordinary life. I continue to uncover stories of her dedication and relentless pursuit of perfection that shaped her into an icon of the ballet world. Despite the passage of time, her legacy endures, reminding me of the indomitable spirit that runs through our veins. This revelation has kindled a renewed passion and respect for the arts within me, as I bask in the radiant glow of my great-grandmother's talent.

C: The secret aristocratic parent

Looking into my family history, I made a captivating discovery that forever altered my perception of where I come from. Unveiled before me was the name of my great grandmother's secret parent, a deliberately hushed truth concealed in the past – a noble aristocrat from a family steeped in grandeur. My mind jumps to extravagant ballrooms adorned with crystal chandeliers, where my ancestor would have gracefully glided through the crowd, representing the epitome of refined elegance. I imagine her secret parent, a mysterious figure draped in stunning silks, effortlessly commanding the attention of all who crossed their path. As I dig deeper into this secret connection, fragments of a hidden narrative emerge. Whispers of forbidden love paint a vivid picture of times gone by. This revelation fills me with a newfound appreciation for the complexity of our family's tapestry, where unspoken bonds often bear the most profound impact.

D: The Scottish chieftain

In my quest to trace the origins of my family, I unearthed a gem that took me to the rugged highlands of Scotland. Within the faded pages of our ancestral records, I discovered a name that evoked images of warriors in kilts and ancient castles – a Scottish chief. My heart swelled with pride as I uncovered the rich heritage of my Scottish ancestors. The name of the chieftain echoed through history, symbolising strength, honour and a deep connection to the land. Immersing myself in the traditions and customs of the Scottish clans, I began to embrace my newfound identity. The haunting sound of bagpipes seemed to resonate in my veins, while the vibrant tartan patterns spoke of a legacy that spanned centuries. It was as if I was walking along the same rugged terrain that my ancestors once called home, to breathe in the crisp Highland air and feel the whisper of ancient spirits. The discovery of this Scottish chieftain in my family history has ignited a desire within me to reconnect with my roots and explore the traditions and folklore that shaped our family's story.

E: The famous scientist

As I embarked on my genealogical voyage, I unravelled a tale of brilliance hidden within the branches of my family tree. It was revealed that my great-grandfather, whose name has long been forgotten by the passing of time, was a pioneering scientist whose ground-breaking discoveries had reshaped the scientific world. The pages of history unveiled his tireless pursuit of knowledge and the profound impact of his work. From laboratory notes filled with intricate equations to prizes bestowed upon him by esteemed institutions, his contributions had an impact in many scientific circles. His name became synonymous with innovation and intellectual curiosity. Being immersed in the world of science myself, I am captivated by the sheer magnitude of his achievements. I find solace in knowing that the relentless pursuit of truth courses through my veins, a legacy that inspires me to explore the unknown and push the boundaries of human understanding. This revelation has given me a renewed appreciation for the transformative power of scientific inquiry.

Cambridge C2 Proficiency Reading — Answer sheet

Name _____   Date _____

Part 5
Mark the appropriate answer.

| 0 | A ☐ | B ☐ | C ■ | D ☐ |

31	A ☐	B ☐	C ☐	D ☐
32	A ☐	B ☐	C ☐	D ☐
33	A ☐	B ☐	C ☐	D ☐
34	A ☐	B ☐	C ☐	D ☐
35	A ☐	B ☐	C ☐	D ☐
36	A ☐	B ☐	C ☐	D ☐

Part 6
Add the appropriate answer.

| 37 | 38 | 39 | 40 | 41 | 42 | 43 |

Part 7
Add the appropriate answer.

44	45
46	47
48	49
50	51
52	53

Cambridge C2 Proficiency Reading

Test 8

Part 5

You are going to read an extract from an article. For questions 31–36, mark the appropriate answer (A, B, C or D) that you think fits best according to the text.

Freshers' Week: More Than Just a Week of Revelry

Freshers' Week, as it is known in the UK, is an eagerly anticipated, week-long event that marks the beginning of the university experience for countless students. While it is often associated with having fun, Freshers' Week is about so much more than just that social aspect. Its exact composition will vary from university to university, but it serves as an essential period for students to adapt to their new environment, make connections with other students, explore opportunities and familiarise themselves with university life.

During Freshers' Week, universities organise a diverse range of activities and events to engage and welcome incoming students. These may include campus tours, information sessions, student societies fairs, academic workshops, sports trials and social gatherings. Campus tours help new students navigate the expansive university grounds so as to ensure that they are able to find their way around lecture halls, libraries and other essential facilities. Information sessions provide crucial details on academic programmes, advice for those looking for part-time work alongside their studies, support services and campus policies.

Moreover, student societies' fairs allow students to explore various clubs, societies and interest groups, fostering their involvement in extra-curricular activities. These societies offer platforms for personal and professional growth, enabling students to develop leadership skills, pursue hobbies and make lifelong friends, and not just social media friends. Though extra-curricular activities may seem trivial, they can help students to find like-minded individuals who share their interests, leading to the formation of supportive friendships and creating a sense of community within the university.

Academic workshops during Freshers' Week equip students with study strategies, time-management skills and tips for adapting to the demands of university-level education that they may not have learned at school. These events collectively ensure a holistic introduction to university life, empowering students to make informed choices and make the most of their academic and social experiences.

From a pastoral point of view, Freshers' Week holds immense importance for students transitioning into university life. It provides an opportunity for new students to overcome any feelings of anxiety or homesickness. By engaging in a welcoming and inclusive environment, students can build connections with their peers and establish a support network, which is likely to prove invaluable during their university journey. Freshers' Week helps to foster a sense of belonging, enabling students to feel more comfortable and confident in their new surroundings.

Freshers' Week also exposes students to the numerous resources and opportunities available on campus. It allows them to familiarise themselves with academic support services, career counselling and wellness programmes. By taking advantage of these resources early on, students can proactively seek help and guidance, enhancing their chances of academic success and personal development throughout their university years.

Opinions on the relevance and usefulness of Freshers' Week may vary among the public. While some perceive it as a mere excuse for bad behaviour, others recognise its greater purpose. One perspective is that Freshers' Week predominantly revolves around excessive partying. These individuals argue that the focus on social events distracts students from their academic responsibilities and can lead to unhealthy habits. They believe that universities should instead allocate more time and resources to academic orientations and workshops, ensuring that students are adequately prepared for the challenges ahead.

Conversely, many students view Freshers' Week as an essential period for personal growth and social integration. They emphasise the importance of socialising and building connections during this initial phase of university life. These students believe that the social aspect of Freshers' Week helps alleviate the stress and pressure associated with starting university. By engaging in social activities, they argue that students can develop interpersonal skills, establish friendships and create a support system that contributes to their overall well-being. They also believe that the opportunity to unwind and have fun away from the scrutiny of academics can actually enhance their focus and motivation when it comes to their academic pursuits.

Additionally, some students appreciate the wide range of opportunities and resources that Freshers' Week presents. They recognise that this period offers a unique chance to join clubs and societies and discover new interests. These students believe that participating in such activities enriches their university experience and contributes to their personal and professional development. They also appreciate the exposure to different opportunities, whether it be in the fields of sports, arts, culture or academia, which can shape their future goals and aspirations.

Test 8

31 It is suggested that the purpose of Freshers' Week is

    A often perceived as being an experience of transition.

    B primarily for students to do personal development work.

    C to provide an experience that is unique for each student.

    D often misunderstood by people outside of university life.

32 Events in Freshers' Week help students to expand their

    A social connections and networks.

    B range of academic interests.

    C understanding of academia.

    D knowledge of possible career paths.

33 How does Freshers' Week help students to feel comfortable at university?

    A through the familiarisation of the busy timetable

    B through the atmosphere the university seeks to create

    C through the holistic nature of the events that take place

    D through the support students receive while making academic choices

34 A criticism of Freshers' Week has been that

    A there isn't enough focus on academic life.

    B there is pressure to make students socialise.

    C the activities that students do are too trivial.

    D the help the university provides to students is tortuous.

35 It is suggested that during Freshers' Week many students appreciate

    A the excuse to just do whatever they want.

    B the exclusive focus on social rather than academic activities.

    C the support they receive from academics at their university.

    D the chance to blow off steam and make friends.

36 The overall impression given of Freshers' Week is that

    A it has been very maligned and misrepresented.

    B it enriches the student experience by providing access to extra-curricular activities.

    C it helps students enjoy the moment rather than develop skills for the future.

    D it prepares students for their future on both an academic and a personal level.

Part 6

You are going to read an extract from a newspaper article. Seven paragraphs have been removed. Select from the paragraphs A–H the one that fits each gap (questions 37–43). There is one extra paragraph that you do not need to use.

A global phenomenon: The rise of K-POP

In recent years, one genre of music has captured the attention of music lovers around the world, breaking language barriers and cultural differences. K-POP, short for Korean Pop, has become a global sensation, captivating audiences with its infectious beats, stunning visuals and jaw-dropping performances. The rise of K-POP has been nothing short of remarkable, and its impact on the global music industry is undeniable.

| 37 | |

However, it was in the late 2000s and early 2010s that K-POP truly began to take off on the global stage. This can be attributed to the emergence of talent agencies like SM Entertainment, YG Entertainment and JYP Entertainment, which played a pivotal role in shaping and promoting K-POP acts. These agencies meticulously trained their artists in singing, dancing and stage presence, fostering a level of professionalism and perfectionism rarely seen in the music industry.

| 38 | |

One of the defining characteristics of K-POP is its emphasis on visuals and performances. K-POP groups are known for their impeccably coordinated dance routines, elaborate music videos, and fashion-forward aesthetics. These carefully crafted productions create a visually stunning experience that captivates viewers and sets K-POP apart from other genres. In addition, K-POP artists often engage in fan interactions through social media, live broadcasts and fan meetings, providing a deep sense of connection with their global fanbase.

| 39 | |

It has even made a significant impact on the market in the USA. K-POP acts have managed to break into the highly competitive American music scene, gaining recognition and amassing a dedicated fanbase. Artists like BTS, BLACKPINK and EXO have not only charted on the Billboard Hot 100 but have also performed on major American television shows and received mainstream media coverage. Their success in the US market has opened doors for other K-POP acts, leading to increased visibility and opportunities for them.

| 40 | |

Despite its undeniable global popularity, K-POP has faced criticism on several fronts. One of the main concerns revolves around the manufactured nature of the genre. K-POP groups are often assembled by talent agencies through rigorous auditions and training processes, prioritising marketability over genuine artistic expression. This has led some critics to argue that K-POP is more about the image and packaging rather than the music itself, raising questions about authenticity and artistic integrity.

| 41 | |

In spite of the criticism of the genre, the future of K-POP looks promising, with even greater opportunities for expansion and influence. K-POP is evolving and diversifying, experimenting with new sounds and concepts. The genre's ability to adapt and incorporate global trends ensures its continued relevance in the ever-changing music landscape. Furthermore, collaborations between K-POP artists and international acts have become more frequent and this has fostered a cultural exchange and opened doors to new markets.

| 42 | |

While the Brits may have had more mainstream recognition in the Western market, K-POP bands have managed to make significant strides and have strong and devoted fanbases that rival those of any Western pop act. The success of K-POP bands demonstrates the global appeal and influence of the genre. Its place in the international music industry now seems to be assured.

| 43 | |

A To understand the meteoric rise of K-POP, you need to consider its history. K-POP emerged in South Korea in the 1990s as a fusion of Western pop music, hip hop and traditional Korean music. Influenced by American and European pop acts such as Michael Jackson and Madonna, as well as the local Korean music scene, K-POP artists began crafting a unique sound that blended catchy melodies with energetic choreography. The first wave of K-POP groups, such as H.O.T and Seo Taiji and Boys, laid the foundation for what was to come.

B It has also been claimed that the emphasis on spectacle and choreography can sometimes result in shallow and formulaic music that lacks depth and innovation. This has led to accusations that K-POP is more focused on commercial success and maintaining a polished image rather than pushing boundaries and exploring new artistic territories.

C The success K-POP has achieved amongst music enthusiasts around the world is undeniably impressive, and its appeal is not limited to its homeland of South Korea. It has spread like wildfire across Asia, Europe, the Americas and beyond. International tours by K-POP groups have sold out arenas and stadiums worldwide, breaking attendance records and generating a fervour rarely seen in the music industry. Social media platforms, particularly Twitter and YouTube, have played a significant role in amplifying K-POP's reach.

D When comparing the success of K-POP bands to that of a group like the British group One Direction, it is important to note that both have achieved remarkable levels of popularity in their own right. One Direction enjoyed immense success in the early 2010s, becoming a global sensation and amassing a massive fan following. Similarly, K-POP bands like BTS have gained a dedicated fanbase worldwide, selling out arenas and stadiums during their international tours.

E The question now is: Will it be possible for K-POP artists and bands to sustain their incredible recent success in the future, or will it prove to be just a flash in the pan, as they say? All the indicators are that as long as industry insiders continue to unearth performers that capture the imagination, and as long as those performers continue to put out records that the public can really connect with, the global community will continue to want to listen to them.

F This has caused some to draw parallels between the impact that K-POP has had in the US and that of British bands in the so-called British Invasion of the 1960s. There, again, music that had its roots in American culture found its way back to that country through the recordings and performances of artists from very different cultural backgrounds. In the 1960s, this embellishment led to the richest and most profound changes in popular music, culture and, eventually, civil rights in the US.

G While K-POP has achieved such a remarkable success, this has not come without its challenges. The intense training regimens and rigorous schedules often take a toll on the mental and physical well-being of K-POP artists. This has sparked discussions about the industry's demanding nature and the need to prioritise the health and welfare of its performers. Additionally, cultural-appropriation controversies and issues of representation have been raised.

H The influence of Western music on K-POP during these formative years cannot be overlooked. K-POP draws inspiration from various genres, including pop, R&B, hip hop, EDM and rock. Collaborations with Western producers and songwriters such as Teddy Riley, will.i.am and Ryan Tedder have helped K-POP artists create songs with an international appeal. This cross-pollination of musical styles has been instrumental in K-POP's success.

Part 7

You are going to read an extract from an article in which five people talk about their favourite car. For questions 44–53, choose from the sections (A–E). The sections may be selected more than once.

In which section are the following mentioned?

how cars can help to make experiences even more memorable	44
how cars can strengthen connections between people	45
going against stereotypes and societal expectations	46
how cars can become a kind of companion to their drivers	47
realising a scenario that someone had fantasised about	48
cars as a symbol of humans' advanced technical achievements	49
a car whose flaws were viewed in a positive light	50
a car that appeals to people with a specific passion	51
the sense of autonomy that cars can give people	52
a car that provided a memorable sensory experience	53

My favourite car

We typically spend a lot of time in our cars, and the cars we own, therefore, end up playing an important role in our lives. Five people tell us about their favourite cars.

A: The family car

My parents' old family car holds a special place in my heart. It was a vintage beauty; a true classic that symbolised countless memories of our family adventures. This elegant vehicle had a timeless charm that surpassed its age, becoming an irreplaceable part of our family's history. Everything about the car was familiar and soothing to me at the same time. It effortlessly carried us on long road trips, its spacious interior providing ample room for my siblings and me to create lasting bonds. The car's vibrant red exterior got a lot of attention wherever we went, sparking conversations and inviting smiles. From the bumpy countryside roads to the scenic coastal drives, our family car withstood the test of time, thus demonstrating its enduring reliability. Its steady rhythm echoed the beat of our collective joy, filling the air with laughter and stories. Every dent and scratch on its body tells a tale, a testament to the adventures we embarked upon together.

B: My first car

Ah, my first car! The very thought of it still fills me with a surge of excitement and nostalgia. It was a modest hatchback, nothing extravagant, but it was a very special to me. As a new driver, the world seemed to open up before me, and that car became my gateway to endless possibilities. I vividly recall the day I received the keys to my own little kingdom on wheels. The sleek silver exterior glistened under the sunlight, and the smell of new upholstery was all around me as I sank into the driver's seat. The engine roared to life with a delightful purr, eagerly awaiting the adventures that lay ahead. From the moment I turned the key, that car became an extension of my personality. It witnessed my triumphs and failures, my laughter and tears. It faithfully carried me to college, work and countless late-night escapades with friends. When I think back to the scratches and dents the car acquired when I was young, I cannot help but smile.

C: The high-performance car

When it comes to high-performance cars, one vehicle stands above the rest in my eyes – the sleek and powerful marvel known as the 'Supreme GT'. This masterpiece of engineering is a true representation of speed, luxury and precision. It represents absolute automotive excellence, capturing the hearts of enthusiasts like me, worldwide. From its aerodynamic curves to its thunderous engine, the Supreme GT exudes an undeniable magnetism. The moment I sat behind the wheel, I was instantly transported into a world of adrenaline-fueled excitement. Whether conquering winding mountain passes or effortlessly overtaking on the open highway, the Supreme GT, for me, remains unrivalled. Its precise handling and lightning-fast acceleration elevate driving to an art form, a dance between man and machine. It responds to my every touch of the pedal and my turn of the wheel with unparalleled grace and agility. But beyond its impressive performance, the Supreme GT represents a symbol of accomplishment and aspiration. It stands as a testament to human ingenuity and engineering prowess.

D: The adapted car

The adapted car that I drive as a person with a disability has transformed my life in countless ways. This remarkable vehicle has allowed me to regain a sense of freedom and independence that I once thought was lost. It is not just a means of transportation; it is my key to unlocking new horizons and pursuing a life without limitations. The adaptations made to this car are nothing short of extraordinary. Every detail has been carefully designed to cater to my specific needs, ensuring that I can navigate the world with ease and confidence. For instance, specialised controls have been created for the car that I am able to reach and operate easily, and the doors and seats have also been modified to allow them to open and move effortlessly. This car is a true testament to human innovation and inclusivity. With the adapted car, I am no longer confined by my disability in ways that some people might expect. I can embark on spontaneous adventures, run errands and engage in social activities without relying on others for assistance. It empowers me to live life on my terms, breaking down barriers and defying societal limitations.

E: The convertible

Picture this – a sleek convertible gliding along the sun-drenched roads of northern Spain, the wind in my hair as the stunning landscape unfolds before my eyes. The experience of driving a convertible had often been present in my day dreams up until now, but then I did actually have the pleasure of driving one such vehicle during a summer holiday in this picturesque region. Exploring the diverse landscapes of northern Spain became a captivating adventure. From the rugged mountains to the charming coastal villages, every destination was infused with a sense of discovery and wonder. But it wasn't just the destination that made this experience unforgettable; it was the sheer joy of the journey itself. With the wind in my hair and the sun on my face, I felt a profound sense of liberation and serenity. The convertible became more than just a car; it was a vessel of unforgettable memories. From sunset drives along the rugged coastline to picnics amidst vineyards, every moment was enhanced by the charm of the convertible.

Cambridge C2 Proficiency Reading

Answer sheet

Name _____   Date _____

Part 5

Mark the appropriate answer.

0	A	B	**C**	D
31	A	B	C	D
32	A	B	C	D
33	A	B	C	D
34	A	B	C	D
35	A	B	C	D
36	A	B	C	D

Part 6

Add the appropriate answer.

37	38	39	40	41	42	43

Part 7

Add the appropriate answer.

44	45
46	47
48	49
50	51
52	53

Answers

Cambridge C2 Proficiency Reading

Test 1

Part 5		Key words from the questions	Clues from the text
31	B	…more often now than they used…	Nowadays, however, locksmiths specialise more and more in automotive locksmithing work, dealing with different types of vehicle locks, including traditional locks as well as 'transponder' and 'smart' locks…
32	D	…staying at school…	Getting a high school diploma or equivalent qualification is typically a good first step. Although not a mandatory requirement, a solid educational foundation can significantly enhance one's understanding of the field.
33	A	…owes his skill as a locksmith…to…	I sought opportunities to work as an apprentice under experienced locksmiths…allowed me to observe and learn from seasoned professionals so as to be able to hone my practical skills and deepen my understanding of real-life scenarios…locksmiths encounter.
34	C	…how much people…pay…'lockouts'?	I don't like to feel that I have the right to demand lots of money, but this part of the job really is what locksmiths earn the majority of their money from.
35	D	…educational aspect…mention?	I often provide expert advice on state-of-the-art security systems and measures to protect homes, businesses or other properties.
36	B	…impression given of the writer…	Being a locksmith is not just about unlocking doors or duplicating keys; it's about being a trusted problem-solver, a reliable source of security advice and a compassionate helper in times of crisis.

Part 6		Key words from the questions	Clues from the text
37	B	…a wide range…These messages span…and driving corporate success.	…utilise this versatile tool to maximise results.
38	D	…offers unparalleled cost-effectiveness.	…at an extremely low cost.
39	H	Personalising content to the profiles and interests of specific users…foster a sense of exclusivity…	…businesses can create highly targeted emails, tailored to each recipient's preferences, behaviour and purchasing history.
40	C	Moreover, compliance with privacy regulations…	…ensure the right balance between making an impact and avoiding the risk of being perceived as unwanted junk mail.
41	A	Email marketing… revolutionised… effectiveness…communicate…customers.	…unprecedented efficiency…enhances customers' engagement and drives sales.
42	F	…keeping in mind likely human reactions to messages…people tend to respond to positively.	…irritating potential customers to the point where they decide to unsubscribe from their company's email notifications.
43	G	…establish meaningful connections with their customers…differentiate a company from its competitors.	…a cohesive and powerful marketing ecosystem that makes a company stand out.

Answers

Part 7		Key words from the questions	Clues from the text
44	C	…question what we assumed was real	Salvador Dalí's 'The Persistence of Memory' is a surrealist masterpiece that challenges the boundaries of reality and perception.
45	B	…a long-lasting artistic legacy	…makes 'Mona Lisa' an enduring masterpiece that continues to captivate audiences and inspire countless artists.
46	A	…painting methods…inspire strong feelings…	…Van Gogh's use of swirling brushstrokes and vibrant colours creates a sense of enchantment and emotional depth.
47	D	art's ability…demonstrate…achieve great things	It represents the Renaissance ideal of humanism, highlighting the belief in the individual's ability to strive for greatness and connection with God.
48	B	…relationship between people and the natural world	'Mona Lisa' represents the epitome of Renaissance art, combining a harmonious balance of naturalism, idealism and symbolism.
49	E	…cry of pain…a brutal world	Picasso's ability to capture the essence of human suffering and his bold expression of outrage make this painting a timeless masterpiece…This painting remains an enduring symbol of protest and a call to action against the atrocities of war.
50	D	…create the feeling that the viewer is inside it	The painting's grand scale and monumental presence further enhance its impact, enveloping the viewer in a spiritual and contemplative experience.
51	C	…art's ability…brief our time is on Earth	They symbolise the transient nature of existence and the futility of trying to control or grasp time. The empty landscape and the distant horizon evoke a sense of desolation and the fragility of human existence.
52	E	…combining art…create a fairer society	Picasso's artistic genius and his constant commitment to social justice have cemented this painting as one of the most significant and influential works of art of the 20th century.
53	A	the artist's ability…represent…dynamism of a subject…techniques…	The artist's use of contrasting colours and energetic brushwork evokes a sense of movement and energy…

Test 2

Part 5		Key words from the questions	Clues from the text
31	B	…writer's experience of playing musical instruments?	Ever since I was a fresh-faced student, I have played the guitar, and prior to that I took piano and violin lessons at school…a guitar because that's the instrument that's closest to my heart…
32	A	How…writer find the course…	I started looking online for a workshop that provided classes in instrument construction in my area, but I started to despair as nothing showed up in the many searches I made and none of my musician friends could help me either. However, I did find the number for a chap called

Cambridge C2 Proficiency Reading

			Tony Marcos who is a luthier.
33	D	…most important thing that the writer learned…design phase?	What really astounded me was discovering that the careful selection of materials, such as spruce wood…
34	C	…which part…process can violin builders express themselves artistically?	…the selection of varnish and its application to the wood to preserve it and make it shine demands technical expertise and a sense of how to make objects look attractive.
35	D	…writer's teacher react to the completion…instrument?	He did give me some good advice on improving the sound, but he was kind enough to wait until the next class, and just let me appreciate what I had achieved for a couple of days.
36	B	How…writer feel…end of the course?	…I would say that what we learned was just the tip of the iceberg in terms of the knowledge and skills necessary to pursue their passion for violin making professionally.

Part 6		Key words from the questions	Clues from the text
37	F	With an insatiable thirst for knowledge and a devotion to automobiles, Mark's passion for cars had emerged at a very early stage and stayed with him for decades to come.	…how his constant love for cars unfolded into his dream job…
38	B	…Mark's path intersected with individuals who owned exquisite and luxurious cars at a young age.	…formative years that his appreciation for performance and precision took root, setting the stage for his future endeavours.
39	D	Acquiring all this knowledge and hearing so many fascinating stories inspired Mark to share his own experiences and insights.	…I was a bit obsessed with it, really. I just loved knowing everything about a car."
40	G	As Mark's career soared…	…captivated viewers and propelled him to become a sought-after automotive personality.
41	A	Throughout his illustrious career…	…test a new car…I would turn up for the test…Among the remarkable cars he has driven…
42	C	His dedication to the technological and emotional aspects of driving have allowed him to excel in his craft.	…engineering brilliance, combined with the emotional connection it creates with the driver, embodies the true essence of automotive passion."
43	H	…and this is the message he seeks to communicate.	…to provide valuable information to assist consumers in making informed decisions about their dream machines.

Part 7		Key words from the questions	Clues from the text
44	D	…timeframe…people being on Mars	…preliminary plans suggest that human missions may occur within the next two to three decades.
45	E	…technical requirements…need…fulfilled…achieve a goal	Successful colonisation would only be possible if there were sustainable life-support systems, efficient resource utilisation… negative effects of the hostile Martian environment…radiation and extreme temperatures.
46	A	…another planet…affect…happens on Earth	…its movements were believed to hold divine messages and influence human affairs.

Answers

47	C	attempts…establish…how feasible…people to live on Mars	…test technologies for future explorative missions that could involve colonisation.
48	D	plans…analyse geological samples from Mars on Earth	…collect samples gathered by the Perseverance rover and return them to Earth, enabling detailed laboratory examination…
49	B	artistic representations of life on Mars	From H.G. Wells' *War of the Worlds* to Ray Bradbury's *The Martian Chronicles,* Mars became a backdrop for thrilling tales of alien civilisations, daring expeditions and encounters with extra-terrestrial beings.
50	A	…ancient religious connections…	The name 'Mars' has its origins in ancient Roman mythology.
51	E	…factors affecting the chances of achieving a scientific goal	…chances of success ultimately depend on addressing critical factors.
52	B	…showing that a long-held belief about Mars…not true	…this scientific approach may have disappointed alien hunters…
53	C	…rock formations on Mars…planet's composition	…experiments to analyse the Martian soil and search for signs of life.

Test 3

Part 5		Key words from the questions	Clues from the text
31	C	…original purpose of The Waverley?	…to provide pleasure cruises along the Firth of Clyde… embodied the spirit of adventure and romance that Scott's literary works so elegantly captured.
32	C	…not conformed with people's expectations?	…this paddle steamer defied the odds, sailing on to become the last seagoing paddle steamer in the world.
33	A	…what are the passengers on The Waverley yearning for?	… inspiring a sense of nostalgia as it reminds people of a simpler age where the pace of life was much slower and there seemed to be more time to simply enjoy oneself.
34	C	…happened after the appearance of a notorious bird?	It became a popular on-board pastime, with passengers eagerly scanning the horizon in anticipation of the notorious gull.
35	B	…the Waverley's greatest achievement is	…the Waverley has covered an astonishing distance, equivalent to circling the Earth over 40 times. This unique and remarkable achievement truly highlights…
36	B	…feature of the Waverley most appeals to the writer?	For me, the most heart-warming thing is the memories this piece of Scottish history evokes.

Part 6		Key words from the questions	Clues from the text
37	C	Under the camera lenses and amidst the magnificent setting of the coronation venue…	…Westminster Abbey, captivated the attention of princes and princesses, world leaders, celebrities and millions of spectators worldwide.

Cambridge C2 Proficiency Reading

38	H	Inside the awe-inspiring magnificent coronation hall, which was filled with beautiful decorations and illuminated by countless chandeliers…	This all created an atmosphere of anticipation and reverence.
39	A	In his coronation speech, the delivery of which is also part of an ancient royal tradition…	The crown symbolises the continuity of the monarchy, connecting the present sovereign with kings and queens who have come before.
40	F	The words of the monarch are a reminder of his role as the head of state in the United Kingdom…	I pledge to uphold the principles of democracy, sustainability, and compassion as we strive to build a better world for generations to come."
41	G	The coronation of King Charles III was not only about the royal family and the support they offer to each other on special occasions…	The presence of other members of the royal family…reinforced the royal family's unity and dedication to their role as representatives of the nation.
42	B	Despite these efforts, it would be foolish to assume that everyone in the United Kingdom is wholeheartedly behind the monarchy…	His commitment to public service, charitable undertakings and support for cultural and educational institutions positions him as a figurehead who can inspire and drive forward positive change within the UK.
43	E	With the coronation of King Charles III, the United Kingdom embarks on a new era with a sense of togetherness…	…captured the essence of unity and shared celebration, as the nation stood together to welcome a new chapter in its history.

Part 7		Key words from the questions	Clues from the text
44	D	…technology, amongst other things, to compare food items	I am not only limited to physical stores but also love the convenience and accessibility of online platforms. By making use of the internet, I can effortlessly compare prices across various retailers…
45	E	…structured and conscious food preparation	… involves carefully designing and organising your meals for a specific period of time, such as a week or a month.
46	A	…need to know how to avoid food-related illnesses	My commitment to freeganism requires a keen eye for understanding the difference between spoiled food and food that can be eaten…
47	D	…lack of loyalty to one particular food retailer	Rather than succumbing to the convenience of shopping at a single store, I enjoy the adventure of exploring multiple establishments in pursuit of the best deals and the most favourable prices.
48	B	…greatest financial benefits…used long-term	Such careful planning translates into tangible monetary savings that accumulate over time…
49	C	…not needing to devote as much time to food shopping as…otherwise would	…also reduce the frequency of my shopping trips, which saves me both time and money.
50	C	…psychological effects of using a specific method	… rewards of my bulk-buying endeavours are, above all, enhanced cost efficiency and peace of mind.
51	B	…using information from a combination of print materials and the internet	My tireless efforts in looking through newspapers, magazines and online platforms enable me to benefit from numerous discounts, special offers and promotional deals.
52	A	…distribution of food amongst a connected group of people	…fosters a profound sense of belonging to a community of freegans who stay in touch with and support each other.

Answers

| 53 | E | ...combat the additional expense of spontaneous purchases | ...it helps to eliminate the costs associated with impulsive purchases... |

Test 4

Part 5		Key words from the questions	Clues from the text
31	D	...Taekwondo...it helps practitioners to	...great emphasis on the development of character, fostering values such as courtesy, integrity, perseverance, self-control and indomitable spirit.
32	A	...more energetic fighter not necessarily triumph...Judo?	...the principle of using an opponent's energy against them.
33	A	...problem-solving skills useful...BJJ?	...learn a comprehensive set of moves where you lock your opponent into one position or hold their throat or you use escape tactics to manipulate your opponent's body and prevent them from attacking you.
34	C	...most significant difference between Karate and Taekwondo...	...through strong punches and kicks, focusing on delivering devastating blows to their opponents. Taekwondoists, on the other hand, prioritise speed, flexibility and agility, and employ kicks and rapid footwork to maintain distance and overwhelm their opponents.
35	D	...Judo and BJJ practitioners both do?	...share a common ground in grappling techniques...
36	B	...sets Karate apart...	With its roots in ancient martial traditions...

Part 6		Key words from the questions	Clues from the text
37	H	The ambiguity lies in the diverse perspectives...	...often respected as heroes in some regions, have been condemned as criminals in others.
38	C	...from the Spanish perspective, these actions constituted piracy and acts of aggression against their empire.	To the English, he embodied the spirit of adventure and of the expansion of England's influence overseas.
39	G	...another fascinating example of the contrasting interpretations of his actions in a similar way to Drake.	...this complexity that fuels the debate surrounding his legacy, leaving us with a more complex understanding of his place in history.
40	B	However, their status as a patriot was not universally recognised. The Spanish, whose vessels this figure had often targeted, continued to view him as a pirate.	The two sides of Lafitte's activities add a layer of complexity to his character and makes it less clear whether he was a pirate or patriot.
41	A	...from the perspective of the English, this person was a pirate who posed a threat to their control over Ireland.	Her resistance against the English crown and her diplomatic efforts to protect her family's lands in the face of colonial expansion made her popular amongst the Irish people.
42	F	...examples given here provide valuable insights into the challenges of categorising	This person's legacy as both a pirate and patriot highlights the complexity of historical figures and the way

Cambridge C2 Proficiency Reading

		historical figures as either pirates or patriots.	in which can combine heroic resistance and criminal activities.
43	E	…exploring these stories, we are reminded that historical figures are not easily confined to simplistic labels.	…different interpretations emerge based on one's point of view.

Part 7		Key words from the questions	Clues from the text
44	E	…understanding of people's needs and feelings	… enhance your empathy and respect for the diverse perspectives and backgrounds of the individuals who may come before you in court.
45	D	…keep up to date with changes…of law	…staying up-to-date with legal developments…
46	A	…work hard while you are in compulsory education	…you will need to dedicate yourself to your academic studies at school from a young age…
47	E	…not underestimating the burden of duty…	…remember that the role of a judge is one of immense responsibility and influence.
48	B	…highly rated in your academic studies	Strive to achieve a good grade in your first degree, as academic excellence is highly regarded in the judicial selection process.
49	C	…importance of taking a higher degree at university	Consider pursuing a postgraduate law degree, such as a Master of Law…
50	B	…undertaking voluntary work	…participate in legal societies and debating competitions, and undertake unpaid work to help vulnerable people.
51	A	…need…undertake activities outside of your studies from a young age	…through participation in debates and other non-academic activities.
52	C	…need… show…not biased or easily influenced	Embody and cultivate impartiality, ensuring that personal beliefs, biases or affiliations do not compromise your ability to deliver fair and just decisions.
53	D	…need…remain intellectually curious	Develop your intellectual capabilities…

Test 5

Part 5		Key words from the questions	Clues from the text
31	B	…Pemberton change Coca-Cola's formula…early years?	…with the introduction of prohibition laws in the USA, Pemberton had to modify his formula to remove the alcohol.
32	D	…change…Coca-Cola's approach to business…under new leadership?	Under Candler's leadership, Coca-Cola experienced rapid growth and expansion. To boost sales, Candler introduced innovative marketing strategies…
33	A	…decisive role…helping Coca-Cola establish a wider presence?	…The Coca-Cola Company's global expansion began in the early 20th century when the company began selling licenses to bottle its drinks to other companies.

Answers

34	B	…product…communication problems between branches…World War II?	…World War II, for instance, Coca-Cola's German operations were cut off from the parent company in the United States. Max Keith, the head of Coca-Cola's German branch, devised a new drink using available ingredients, which became known as Fanta.
35	D	…lesson…Coca-Cola…introducing…new drink…late 20th Century?	This episode highlighted the power of consumer loyalty and the significance of preserving a brand's heritage.
36	B	…recent change…Coca-Cola …in response to changing consumer preferences?	Recognising the growing demand for healthier drinks options, the company has expanded its product range to include low-calorie and sugar-free alternatives.

Part 6		Key words from the questions	Clues from the text
37	G	…explore the potential of these innovations to enhance productivity, reduce environmental impact and promote sustainable farming practices.	…understanding of how technological advancements are revolutionising the agricultural landscape.
38	B	…making the achievement of such aims more difficult, yet more important.	…increased efficiency, productivity and sustainability.
39	E	…assist in making informed decisions about the necessary measures and amounts…	…precise application of fertilisers and pesticides, reducing waste and improving resource management.
40	F	An area that tends to be less complicated legally and ethically…	…address issues such as patent protection, intellectual property rights and potential ecological risks associated with the use of GM crops.
41	H	…the implementation of such automated methods necessitates careful consideration of factors such as cost-effectiveness, compatibility with existing infrastructure and technical expertise.	…ensuring the efficient allocation of water resources, automated irrigation systems contribute to water conservation and sustainability in farming.
42	D	Once confrontation has been replaced by cooperation between these various stakeholders…	…bridge the gap between farmers, consumers and policymakers, fostering informed decision-making and promoting dialogue.
43	C	Agricultural innovation undoubtedly has many different aspects…	…multidisciplinary collaborations involving scientists, policymakers, farmers and consumers are crucial to navigating the ethical implications of agricultural innovations.

Part 7		Key words from the questions	Clues from the text
44	C	…confronted by an uncomfortable truth	…Lear confronts the harsh realities of his own stupidity.
45	E	…appreciation of a character's contradiction of society's expectations…	…hold her own in a world dominated by men make her a timeless and empowering figure…
46	A	…having to work hard to portray a character despite having done it many times	The role continues to challenge and inspire me…
47	D	…appreciation of how their character can behave in many different ways	What sets Hamlet apart is his multi-dimensionality…

Cambridge C2 Proficiency Reading

48	A	…significant change in the personality and behaviour of a character	…relished the challenge of capturing Macbeth's transformation from a brave and noble warrior to a ruthless tyrant dealing with feelings of guilt.
49	E	…go beyond conventional gender boundaries	She is a woman unafraid to speak her mind and challenge norms and expectations in society.
50	D	…way to access what is going on in the mind…	…Bringing this extensive inner life to the stage…
51	C	…linguistic complexities of a character's speeches	The poetic richness of his speeches, particularly during the emotional moments of self-reflection, gives me the opportunity to connect with the audience on a deeper level.
52	E	…amusing back-and-forth…	The dialogue between Beatrice and Benedick is a delight to perform, as they shoot comments at each other, like two tennis players passing a ball.
53	B	…experiences remorse	…a tormented soul consumed by guilt is a true acting challenge.

Test 6

Part 5		Key words from the questions	Clues from the text
31	D	…made Martin want to move to London?	My heart was set on London – a fascinating city of dreams…
32	A	Martin's first weeks in London…	The initial thrill of being in London soon started to wear off and reality began to set in.
33	B	…Martin account for his change in artistic direction?	…completely amazed by the spectacle. As the show came to an end, I approached the performer, my heart pounding with excitement.
34	C	…Martin stood out as a street performer because he	…he was intrigued by my 'charisma' and talent as a performer.
35	A	Martin's career…characterised…	With the advice and support of the talent agent, I secured a spot on a popular television talent show…Offers poured in from all directions…
36	B	The impression Martin gives…	…I have never forgotten my humble beginnings.

Part 6		Key words from the questions	Clues from the text
37	B	The study of such prehistoric humans is an exciting and evolving field of research…	We aim to shed light on the fascinating story of our ancestry as humans.
38	A	…leading to the evolution of these multiple human species.	…the emergence of multiple human species, each with unique anatomical and behavioural characteristics.
39	C	Indeed, the discovery of ancient DNA has revolutionised our understanding of the genetic interactions between early humans	…highlighting the link between our species and our extinct relatives.

Answers

		and prehistoric humans.	
40	G	It would be a mistake to assume that prehistoric humans lived stationary lives as the evidence suggests that they could be extremely mobile.	The scale of their movement that this discovery represents serves to highlight the complex interactions between different groups of humans.
41	H	This former species demonstrates that some prehistoric humans possessed both ape-like and human-like characteristics.	…The diverse range of species, such as *Australopithecus sediba*, Neanderthals and the Denisovans, challenge our preconceived notions of a linear progression and highlight the intricate web of human evolution.
42	E	…genetic studies, particularly those by Green (2010) and Reich (2011), have revealed fascinating insights into the genetic legacy of prehistoric humans that we also still experience the impact of today.	This finding further highlights the need to remove any clear dividing line between our species and our extinct cousins.
43	D	As research continues to uncover new fossils, refine dating techniques and utilise advanced genomic analyses, our understanding of prehistoric humans will undoubtedly continue to evolve.	…the dynamic nature of human evolution and the complexities of interactions between different species of prehistoric humans.

Part 7		Key words from the questions	Clues from the text
44	D	…different treatment that artists and crew receive	Bands typically travel in a private jet or a fleet of chartered planes to ensure efficiency and comfort. The crew and equipment, meanwhile, are transported via a fleet of trucks, which may number anywhere from 10 to 30…
45	B	…determining likely levels of interest in the shows amongst the public	Factors like market demand, fan base and historical ticket-sales data help in shaping the tour itinerary.
46	B	…business deals…so a concert can be staged in a specific location	Negotiations with venue management involve securing dates, contract agreements and analysing the infrastructure…
47	E	…balancing of income and outgoings	On average, a stadium world tour can cost tens of millions of dollars. Revenue generation primarily comes from ticket sales…
48	A	…considerations…planning a show	Embarking on a stadium world tour is a colossal undertaking that requires meticulous planning…
49	D	…how artists publicise their shows	Bands work closely with marketing teams and promoters to generate buzz and awareness through traditional and digital channels.
50	C	…potentially fatal consequences of inadequate preparations	AC/DC's 'Razors Edge' world tour experienced a devastating incident in Salt Lake City, Utah, where a combination of poor planning and a tragic accident led to the deaths of three fans.
51	E	…importance of liaising with local authorities	Close collaboration with local law enforcement and venue security staff is crucial in implementing comprehensive security measures…
52	C	…need to follow specifications	Bands work closely with production companies specialising in live events to design and execute these intricate setups.

Cambridge C2 Proficiency Reading

| 53 | A | …need to coordinate the location of concerts effectively | …plan their tours carefully, considering factors such as geographic location, transportation logistics and venue availability. |

Test 7

Part 5		Key words from the questions	Clues from the text
31	C	…the fact that Jeff Buckley's father was a musician	His father's experimental folk-rock style clearly left a lasting impression on him as he received so much exposure to it in his formative years. Guitar virtuosos such as Jimi Hendrix and Jimmy Page inspired his own exploration of the instrument and had the advantage of being somewhat set apart from his home environment.
32	A	…the impact of Buckley's move to New York on his career?	…began to further develop his own musical identity that appealed to music executives. It was during this time that he caught the attention of legendary record executive Steve Berkowitz…
33	C	…Buckley's peers agree…	Thom Yorke of Radiohead once remarked, "Jeff Buckley was an extraordinary musician and a truly gifted songwriter. His work had a profound influence on me, and I know he inspired countless others as well." Chris Martin of Coldplay echoed these sentiments, saying, "Jeff Buckley's music was like a revelation … his artistry pushed the boundaries of what was possible."
34	D	…if Buckley hadn't died prematurely, he would have	…we will never know what music Buckley would have gone on to make had he lived longer, but all the indications are that he had not yet reached the peak of his musical powers.
35	C	…Buckley's influence has endured due to	His voice and guitar playing continue to inspire awe and reverence after his death, serving as a constant reminder of the power of music to connect with the deepest corners of the human spirit.
36	B	The writer's overall impression…	Jeff Buckley's music has a kind of other-worldly quality to it, as if he had been more than a mere mortal somehow.

Part 6		Key words from the questions	Clues from the text
37	C	…one such example of these kinds of collective struggles…	…the indomitable spirit of those fighting for their rights and the recognition of their collective power.
38	A	While political figures acknowledged the importance of education and the need for change, concrete policy actions remained elusive.	…offered a platform for demonstrators to voice their grievances, amplifying their concerns and generating public discourse.
39	G	This demonstration received a mixed response from the public and the media.	…'Our Planet, Our Responsibility' and 'The Time for Change is Now' filled the skyline, capturing the essence of the protesters' demands.
40	D	…which was, in contrast, more of an inward-	… engaging in acts of civil disobedience and creating international solidarity to exert pressure on the

Answers

		looking movement.	authorities.
41	F	This insubordination led to heightened tensions on the streets of Paris.	…resisted the demands put forth by the protesters, often resorting to tactics aimed at undermining collective bargaining efforts.
42	H	What distinguishes these demonstrations is the ability of the protesters to use the power of public opinion and media attention.	…signal a collective awakening, as citizens recognise the power of unity and activism.
43	E	These ongoing demonstrations also highlight the tension and conflict that arise…	…increase the determination of the demonstrators, as they recognise that the fight for their rights is far from over.

Part 7		Key words from the questions	Clues from the text
44	C	…deliberately kept under wraps	…a deliberately hushed truth concealed in the past…
45	B	…achieved international fame	Her enchanting performances had captivated audiences on grand stages across the globe.
46	E	…helped to expand people's knowledge	…was a pioneering scientist whose ground-breaking discoveries had reshaped the scientific world.
47	A	…actions…powered by strong emotions	…my ancestor, plagued by envy, had ruthlessly taken the life of his business partner in a fit of rage.
48	D	…feeling of being transported to a specific place	…as if I was walking along the same rugged terrain that my ancestors once called home…
49	D	…new sense of belonging to a specific culture	…has ignited a desire within me to reconnect with my roots and explore the traditions and folklore that shaped our family's story.
50	A	…surprise that an ancestor's character traits had not resurfaced	…I can't help but wonder how such a malevolent streak could be concealed within the depths of our family history.
51	E	…shared an interest that the writer already had	Being immersed in the world of science myself, I am captivated by the sheer magnitude of his achievements.
52	B	…discovery that led to the writer to appreciate something more	This revelation has kindled a renewed passion and respect for the arts within me…
53	C	…discovery…evokes images of luxury	My mind jumps to images of extravagant ballrooms adorned with crystal chandeliers…

Test 8

Part 5		Key words from the questions	Clues from the text
31	D	…purpose of Freshers' Week…	…While it is often associated with having fun, Freshers' Week is about so much more than just that social aspect.
32	A	Events in Freshers' Week help students to expand…	…student societies' fairs allow students to explore various clubs, societies and interest groups, fostering their involvement in extra-curricular activities.

Cambridge C2 Proficiency Reading

33	B	… Freshers' Week help all students to feel comfortable at university?	…By engaging in a welcoming and inclusive environment, students can build connections with their peers and establish a support network…
34	A	…a criticism… Freshers' Week…	Opinions on the relevance and usefulness of Freshers' Week may vary among the public. While some perceive it as a mere excuse for bad behaviour, others recognise its greater purpose.
35	D	…during Freshers' Week many students appreciate	…the opportunity to unwind and have fun away from the scrutiny of academics can actually enhance their focus and motivation when it comes to their academic pursuits.
36	D	…overall impression… Freshers' Week..	…participating in such activities enriches their university experience and contributes to their personal and professional development.

Part 6		Key words from the questions	Clues from the text
37	A	To understand the meteoric rise of K-POP…	…nothing short of remarkable, and its impact on the global music industry is undeniable.
38	H	The influence of Western music on K-POP during these formative years…	…fostering a level of professionalism and perfectionism rarely seen in the music industry.
39	C	The success K-POP has achieved amongst music enthusiasts around the world is undeniably impressive…	…fan interactions through social media, live broadcasts and fan meetings, providing a deep sense of connection with their global fanbase.
40	F	This has caused some to draw parallels between the impact that K-POP has had in the US and that of British bands in the so-called British Invasion of the 1960s.	Their success in the US market has opened doors for other K-POP acts, leading to increased visibility and opportunities for them.
41	B	It has also been claimed that the emphasis on spectacle and choreography…	…more about the image and packaging rather than the music itself, raising questions about authenticity and artistic integrity.
42	D	When comparing the success of K-POP bands to that of a group like the British group One Direction…	…collaborations between K-POP artists and international acts have become more frequent and this has fostered a cultural exchange and opened doors to new markets.
43	G	While K-POP has achieved such a remarkable success…	Its place in the international music industry now seems to be assured.

Part 7		Key words from the questions	Clues from the text
44	E	…cars…help…make experiences even more memorable	…every moment was enhanced by the charm of the convertible.
45	A	…cars…strengthen connections between people	…its spacious interior providing ample room for my siblings and me to create lasting bonds.
46	D	…going against stereotypes and societal expectations	With the adapted car, I am no longer confined by my disability in ways that some people might expect.
47	B	…cars…kind of companion to their drivers	…that car became an extension of my personality.

Answers

48	E	realising a scenario…fantasised about	The experience of driving a convertible had often been present in my day dreams up until now…
49	C	cars…symbol of humans' advanced technical achievements	It represents absolute automotive excellence…
50	A	…car…flaws…viewed…positive light	Every dent and scratch on its body tells a tale, a testament to the adventures we embarked upon together.
51	C	…car…appeals to people…specific passion	…capturing the hearts of enthusiasts like me, worldwide.
52	D	…sense of autonomy…cars…give people	…it is my key to unlocking new horizons and pursuing a life without limitations.
53	B	…car…memorable sensory experience	The sleek silver exterior glistened under the sunlight, and the smell of new upholstery was all around me as I sank into the driver's seat.

Bonus material

The following content is taken from:

Part 1

For questions 1–8, read the text below and decide which answer best fits each gap. In the separate answer sheet, mark the appropriate answer (A, B, C or D).

Guitar Hero

Sony Playstation's *Guitar Hero* game has been **(1)**_____ a true phenomenon by gamers and music enthusiasts alike. This rhythm-based video game provides an **(2)**_____ experience in that players can simulate playing a guitar or other musical instruments using a specialised controller shaped like a guitar. *Guitar Hero* has **(3)**_____ players all over the world who cannot get enough of it.

One of the key features of *Guitar Hero* is the inclusion of a wide range of songs that allow players to discover new artists and **(4)**_____ how they make their music. The gameplay revolves around hitting notes accurately as they appear on the screen, mimicking the experience of playing a real instrument. The difficulty level gradually increases and, with a little **(5)**_____, players can invariably step up their timing and coordination to reflect this heightened complexity.

Not only has *Guitar Hero* been able to create a feeling of being drawn into the music from the **(6)**_____ of the player, its 'multiplayer mode' has also allowed gamers to play with their friends **(7)**_____, thus adding a social element to the experience.

Were it not for the lure of real guitar playing, interest in *Guitar Hero* would be minimal and it cannot be said to have replaced real instrument practice. Nevertheless, it is capable of inspiring aspiring musicians to pick up a musical instrument and gives them the momentum required to make **(8)**_____ as a live musician.

1	A	embraced	B	deemed	C	portrayed	D	speculated
2	A	explicit	B	indirect	C	immersive	D	exaggerated
3	A	supplemented	B	succumbed	C	seduced	D	summoned
4	A	appreciate	B	initiate	C	conceive	D	formulate
5	A	perseverance	B	morale	C	credibility	D	accumulation
6	A	stance	B	transmission	C	possession	D	perspective
7	A	subconsciously	B	conclusively	C	collaboratively	D	voluntarily
8	A	sense	B	progress	C	way	D	up

Part 2

For questions 9–16, read the text below and decide which word best fits each gap. Use only one word for each gap. In the separate answer sheet, write your answers in capital letters, using one box per letter.

Plastic bags

It was the photographs of sea creatures suffering **(9)**_____ the effects of plastic pollution in their ocean habitats that triggered a sense of discomfort with plastic bag use amongst a significant proportion of the population. What's **(10)**_____, recent research endeavours in the field of marine biology have highlighted the extremely negative impact that plastic has on eco-systems. Members of the public would be foolish to be so short-sighted **(11)**_____ to ignore the threat that plastic bags pose.

Fortunately, there have been some efforts made by governments to stipulate that retailers must charge their customers for plastic bags. Should it **(12)**_____ happen that a customer fails to bring a suitable bag with them, this individual will be obligated to purchase a reusable cloth or paper bag to carry their groceries. **(13)**_____ a consequence of such initiatives, the reusing of plastic bags has become normalised in many countries.

(14)_____ sensible, reusing plastic bags is not always a habit that consumers can accustom themselves to easily. Fostering a culture of responsibility can help to make this clear for everyone. Consequently, educational campaigns have been launched to raise awareness of the environmental impact of plastic bags. These campaigns have a **(15)**_____ purpose: firstly, they reduce the consumption of single-use plastic bags, and secondly, they encourage a shift towards more sustainable habits. In many countries the campaigns have taken **(16)**_____ and have proven to be very successful.

Part 3

For questions 17–24, use the stem word on the right to form the correct word that fills each gap. In the separate answer sheet, write your answers in capital letters, using one box per letter.

Stetson hats

Renowned and revered all over the world, the Stetson Hat Company is an iconic American brand that has become (17)_____ with the Wild West and cowboy culture. Today it seems (18)_____ that a cowboy would wear any other type of headwear.

SYNONYM
CONCEIVE

Established in 1865 by John B. Stetson, the company revolutionised the hat industry with the high quality and (19)_____ of its headwear. No Stetson hat has ever been made that was not crafted using traditional techniques and premium materials.

DURABLE

The Stetson Hat Company saw its popularity surge during the late 19th and early 20th centuries, ultimately becoming the preferred choice for cowboys, farmers and outdoor (20)_____. Its wide brim and high crown give the wearer a distinctive and rugged look, giving rise to the (21)_____ that Stetson wearers are tough and distinguished.

ENTHUSE

PERCEIVE

However, no one should make the (22)_____ that this type of hat is the only one that the Stetson company produces. Over the years, Stetson has expanded its range of hats to cater to different styles and trends. Moreover, it should also be praised for its (23)_____ of traditional hat-making techniques to this day. It is this (24)_____ that distinguishes Stetson hats from those of its competitors.

ASSUME

RETAIN
CRAFT

Part 4

For questions 25–30, complete the second sentence, using the word given, so that it has a similar meaning to the first sentence. Do not change the word provided, and use between three and eight words in total. In the separate answer sheet, write your answers in capital letters, using one box per letter.

25   I'm extremely grateful that you helped me.

   OBLIGED

   I'm _____ your help.

26   Unfortunately, she isn't allowed to tell you that.

   LIBERTY

   She _____ give you that information.

27   The fact that she was falling behind the lead runner did not lessen her determination at all.

   LEAST

   She fell behind, but that didn't discourage her _____.

28   It's fantastic that he remembered to take down the car's registration number.

   PRESENCE

   He _____ write down the car's details.

29   One minute the weather was fine and the next there was a torrential downpour.

   ALL

   It was dry and then _____ it started to rain heavily.

30   The only reason why he passed the exam was because he had tutors.

   WERE

   _____ the tutors, he wouldn't have passed the exam.

Answer sheet: Cambridge C2 Proficiency Use of English

Test No. ☐

Mark out of 36 ☐

Name _____ **Date** _____

Part 1: Multiple choice

8 marks

Mark the appropriate answer (A, B, C or D).

| 0 | A **B** C D |

1	A B C D		5	A B C D
2	A B C D		6	A B C D
3	A B C D		7	A B C D
4	A B C D		8	A B C D

Part 2: Open cloze

8 marks

Write your answers in capital letters, using one box per letter.

| 0 | B | E | C | A | U | S | E | | | |

9.
10.
11.
12.
13.
14.
15.
16.

Part 3: Word formation

8 marks

Write your answers in capital letters, using one box per letter.

17.
18.
19.
20.
21.
22.
23.
24.

Part 4: Key word transformation

12 marks

Write your answers in capital letters, using one box per letter.

25.
26.
27.
28.
29.
30.

Cambridge C2 Proficiency Use of English

Part 1

For questions 1–8, read the text below and decide which answer best fits each gap. In the separate answer sheet, mark the appropriate answer (A, B, C or D).

Home to roost

Keeping chickens can be a rewarding and **(1)**_____ experience for people living in either rural or urban locations. These delightful creatures provide fresh eggs and natural **(2)**_____ control, as well as an opportunity to connect with nature. It is no surprise that chicken-keeping has become such a popular past time, but there are several key aspects that need to be considered when embarking on the journey of raising chickens.

Firstly, suitable housing is essential for the birds' well-being. A secure and spacious coop **(3)**_____ chickens protection from predators, shelter from **(4)**_____ weather conditions and a comfortable roosting area. Additionally, nesting boxes should be provided for egg-laying hens.

A balanced diet is crucial for the health and productivity of chickens. A commercially available chicken feed, formulated to meet their **(5)**_____ needs, serves as the foundation of their diet. Supplemented with kitchen scraps and **(6)**_____ greens, chickens can enjoy a varied and healthy diet.

Regular access to fresh water is also vital. Chickens require a constant supply of clean water to stay hydrated, **(7)**_____ digestion and regulate body temperature. Provision of a water dispenser or shallow dish is recommended on the condition that it remains clean and free from **(8)**_____. Regularly cleaning the coop, removing droppings and providing fresh bedding not only promotes cleanliness but also minimises the risk of parasites and bacteria affecting the chickens.

1	A	intimate	B	enriching	C	compatible	D	versatile
2	A	pest	B	residence	C	tolerance	D	odour
3	A	cultivates	B	transmits	C	conceives	D	affords
4	A	awkward	B	adverse	C	senseless	D	formidable
5	A	characteristic	B	attainable	C	nutritional	D	complementary
6	A	foraged	B	fertile	C	extravagant	D	torrential
7	A	force	B	handle	C	relieve	D	aid
8	A	intolerances	B	famines	C	contaminants	D	inequalities

Part 2

For questions 9–16, read the text below and decide which word best fits each gap. Use only one word for each gap. In the separate answer sheet, write your answers in capital letters, using one box per letter.

Are insects the food of the future?

It's fair to say that insects are not the most appealing of snacks that one can imagine. Many people would turn their noses **(9)**_____ at the prospect of actually eating an insect. Nevertheless, it cannot be denied that many of these creatures are highly nutritious. To be more precise, they're packed **(10)**_____ protein, healthy fats, vitamins and minerals. Incorporating insects into our diets could provide us with a sustainable and efficient source of essential nutrients, especially in regions where access to traditional protein sources is limited. Might such a development really **(11)**_____ about in the foreseeable future?

Insect farming is widely considered to have a significantly lower environmental impact compared to traditional livestock farming. This can be put **(12)**_____ to the fact that insects have a high feed-conversion rate, meaning they can convert feed **(13)**_____ edible protein more efficiently than traditional livestock. As a result, insect farming is a resource-efficient method of food production that could relieve the strain **(14)**_____ global food systems.

Unfortunately, there are cultural barriers to accepting insects as a mainstream food source in many cultures due to cultural biases. **(15)**_____ factor slowing the adoption of insects as food is the fact that safety standards and guidelines need to be in place to address concerns related to potential allergens in insect-derived products. It's **(16)**_____ noting, however, that many of the concerns and challenges associated with insect farming can be addressed through further research, technological advancements and education.

Part 3

For questions 17–24, use the stem word on the right to form the correct word that fills each gap. In the separate answer sheet, write your answers in capital letters, using one box per letter.

Shakespeare's Globe

Having been built on the south bank of the Thames in London in 1599, the original Globe Theatre would go on to host the premieres of many of Shakespeare's renowned plays. This theatre was wooden and open air, and known for its distinctive architecture, specifically its **(17)**_____ design. — **CIRCLE**

(18)_____, the original Globe was destroyed by fire in 1613, but it was rebuilt the following year. The theatre was ultimately closed in 1642 due to the contemporary dominance of Puritans who had a great **(19)**_____ for theatre in general. — **TRAGEDY** / **TASTE**

The creation of a modern replica of the Globe was **(20)**_____ during the 1990s, and it is located near the site of the original theatre. The aim of the reconstruction project was to create a theatre that resembled the original structure as closely as possible so that the public could once again enjoy the performance of Shakespeare's works and even the **(21)**_____ of standing for three hours. The new Globe Theatre opened to the public in 1997, and since then it has served as a popular venue for performances of Shakespearean plays and other productions. — **TAKE** / **COMFORT**

The modern Globe shares many **(22)**_____ with the original design, including a thatched roof, open courtyard and seating in three tiers. It strives to recreate the **(23)**_____ experience of Shakespeare's time and thus allows audiences to experience the plays in a setting that is a vivid **(24)**_____ of the atmosphere of the Elizabethan era. — **CHARACTER** / **THEATRE** / **EVOKE**

Part 4

For questions 25–30, complete the second sentence, using the word given, so that it has a similar meaning to the first sentence. Do not change the word provided, and use between three and eight words in total. In the separate answer sheet, write your answers in capital letters, using one box per letter.

25 It's impossible to predict how long this construction project will take.

   TELLING

   There is _____ will take.

26 John is usually a tolerant person, but he is very annoyed by people playing loud music at night.

   EXCEPTION

   Although he is usually tolerant, John _____ at night.

27 Nobody appreciates it when their hard work is undone by other people.

   KINDLY

   Nobody _____ by other people.

28 We have to save enough money for the expedition and obtain everything we will need for it.

   ONLY

   Not _____, but we will also have to obtain all of the necessary items.

29 Many thousands of kilometres separate them, but German and Japanese cultures have had an influence on each other.

   THOUGH

   _____, German and Japanese cultures have influenced each other.

30 I would be alerted immediately should anyone break into the building.

   EVENT

   In _____, I would receive an alert right away.

**Answer sheet: Cambridge C2 Proficiency
Use of English**

Test No.

Mark out of 36

Name _____   **Date** _____

Part 1: Multiple choice   8 marks

Mark the appropriate answer (A, B, C or D).

| 0 | A **B** C D |

1	A B C D		5	A B C D
2	A B C D		6	A B C D
3	A B C D		7	A B C D
4	A B C D		8	A B C D

Part 2: Open cloze   8 marks

Write your answers in capital letters, using one box per letter.

| 0 | B E C A U S E |

9.
10.
11.
12.
13.
14.
15.
16.

Part 3: Word formation

8 marks

Write your answers in capital letters, using one box per letter.

17.
18.
19.
20.
21.
22.
23.
24.

Part 4: Key word transformation

12 marks

Write your answers in capital letters, using one box per letter.

25.
26.
27.
28.
29.
30.

Cambridge C2 Proficiency Reading

www.ingramcontent.com/pod-product-compliance
Lightning Source LLC
Chambersburg PA
CBHW042019090526
44590CB00029B/4338